Inside the Critics' Circle

PRINCETON STUDIES IN CULTURAL SOCIOLOGY

Paul J. DiMaggio, Michèle Lamont,
Robert J. Wuthnow, and Viviana A. Zelizer,
Series Editors

*For a full list of titles in the series, go to https://press.princeton.edu
/catalogs/series/title/princeton-studies-in-cultural-sociology.html.*

Inside the Critics' Circle

Book Reviewing in Uncertain Times

Phillipa K. Chong

Princeton University Press
Princeton and Oxford

Copyright © 2020 by Princeton University Press

Published by Princeton University Press
41 William Street, Princeton, New Jersey 08540
6 Oxford Street, Woodstock, Oxfordshire OX20 1TR

press.princeton.edu

Library of Congress Control Number: 2019938770
ISBN: 9780691167466
ISBN (e-book): 9780691186030

British Library Cataloging-in-Publication Data is available

Editorial: Meagan Levinson and Jacqueline Delaney
Production Editorial: Ellen Foos
Text and Jacket Design: Chris Ferrante
Production: Erin Suydam
Publicity: Alyssa Sanford and Kathryn Stevens
Copyeditor: Kathleen Kageff

This book has been composed in Gazette LT Std,
Franklin Gothic Std, and ITC Cheltenham Std

Printed on acid-free paper. ∞

Printed in the United States of America

10 9 8 7 6 5 4 3 2 1

For Adam Matak

Contents

Inside the Critics' Circle

Chapter 1

Introduction

OUR PHONE CALL IS CLOSE TO ENDING. It was a great get for the project: an interview-based study exploring how fiction reviewers do the work of evaluating worth.

Not only does the speaker on the other end of the line boast a review career that spans decades, but she has also reviewed for the most important and influential newspapers in North America—and is one of the few people to have once held anything resembling a full-time reviewing gig in today's newspaper landscape. This is someone that, as a social scientist studying evaluation, you want to interview.

Imagine my surprise, then, when this critic casually mentions: "When you say you think of me as a tastemaker—that just makes me kind of laugh." She continues, "It would be lots of fun if I could say, 'Get away from me! I'm a tastemaker!'" like a person of royalty issuing edicts. But this is a far cry from how she sees herself.

And she was not alone.

————————

Book reviewers are examples of market intermediaries: third parties who mediate between producers (writers and publishers) and audiences (readers), and whose interventions shape how the objects under scrutiny (books) subsequently come to be valued.[1]

And book reviews matter. Getting a review in a high-status publication like the *New York Times Book Review*—regardless of whether the review is positive or negative—increases the odds that a writer will go on to publish future books.[2] Furthermore, gaining the attention of reviewers is a first and necessary step to becoming a high-status novelist.[3] Yet, the relevance of book reviewing has been openly questioned.

The health of arts and culture reviewing has long been connected with the fortunes of traditional newspaper media, which have experienced significant decline over the past few decades including dwindling circulation numbers, decreasing advertising revenues, and job cuts. While I was conducting interviews for this project, for instance, the *Los Angeles Times* laid off all nonstaff book reviewers and culled their full-time review staff to only four.[4] Two years later, as I analyzed the interview data, the *Chicago Sun-Times* eliminated its regular book pages.[5] And most recently, as I was pulling together the full draft of this manuscript, the *New York Times*—the last remaining newspaper in North America with a freestanding book review section—announced that the guiding question for their book journalism was shifting from "Does this book merit a *review*?" to "Does this book merit *coverage*?"[6] with the latter suggesting an openness to alternative means of reporting on books. Such changes signal how the function and future of traditional book reviews is being questioned not only in the wider context of news media, but also within book pages themselves.

Accompanying changes within traditional book review sections, the growing visibility of amateur reviewers has spurred interest in the potential declining influence of traditional reviewers. Amateur reviewers are sometimes called "reader-reviewers" to emphasize that their reviews and evaluations are not offered in the context of professional practice, but by private consumers—by readers, for readers.[7] In particular, as blogs, social networking sites (e.g., Goodreads), and online marketplaces (e.g., Amazon.com) enable readers to learn about new books through alternative means, an increasing number of observers are asking: Why should we pay attention to what professional critics have to say when we can get information about books in myriad other spaces? If readers can go to Amazon.com and read fifty layperson reviews of a new book, what need do they have for professional book reviews? And pushed to an extreme position: Why should we care about what anyone else has to say about books if reading preference is just a matter of idiosyncratic taste?

The purpose of this book is not to take sides on debates about whether we should sound the death knell for traditional reviewing, if some people's aesthetic judgments should matter more than others, or whether amateur reviewers are ruining book culture. Instead, I treat such fundamental questions as an intrinsic part of the broader *context of uncertainty* in which critics operate. Critics are acutely aware of the critiques and challenges facing reviewing. My objective is to understand how this context concretely affects the way critics understand and do the work reviewing.

Rather than as full existential or moral panic, I find that critics' sensitivity to the multiple debates about the competence and relevance of contemporary reviews manifested in more quotidian ways. This included people's lack of certainty about whether they were the "right" people for me to interview for the book project when they didn't hold a full-time reviewing position (few people do). It also manifested in the way respondents described their review process: the doubt, moral quandaries, professional anxieties, and yes, fears for the future of book culture, which constrained how they inhabited the role of reviewer.

I offer a detailed portrait of book reviewing from the perspective of reviewers, including how they cope with the uncertainties peculiar to the practice of literary evaluation. Far from an image of powerful tastemakers issuing edicts, the critics I interviewed experience a great deal of vulnerability while performing the work of reviewing. And by focusing on how critics respond to the broader context of uncertainty surrounding their practices, what becomes evident are the wide range of influences shaping how critics produce reviews— extending well beyond the pages of the books they read.

The Study of Critics

Why study critics at all? After all, research has shown that the more ratings books receive from reader-reviewers in places like Goodreads or Amazon, the greater the odds that it will appear on the *New York Times* best-seller list—while the amount of attention a book received in newspapers has little effect[8]. If the *impact* of book reviews is reducible to sales, such studies could be used to suggest that traditional book reviews no longer matter.

Yet, it is not necessarily the case that the commercial success of a book should be the most salient indicator of a critic's impact or significance. The cultural field has been described as the "economic world reversed" in the sense that economic success is secondary— if not anathema—to concerns of artistic legitimacy (e.g., winning prestigious literary prizes).[9] Indeed, there is evidence that the idea that book reviews should be used for marketing or selling books is at odds with the professional ideology of arts journalists, especially book critics.[10] Critics' sense of professional value, then, and our own estimation of their worth need not be anchored in book sales. Book reviews are about more than just recommending or not recommending commodities for purchase. They are also about conferring artistic legitimacy.

Adjacent to the tastemaker idea, scholars conceptualize reviewers as cultural *consecrators*,[11] whose reviews effectively demarcate which books are worth knowing about—and which are not. Consecration, a religious metaphor, was extended to the cultural field by sociologist Pierre Bourdieu to refer to the process and practices by which social entities are demarcated as belonging to the sacred or to the profane.[12] As cultural consecrators, critics have traditionally been imbued with the authority to demarcate art from non-art, or legitimate from illegitimate cultural offerings. And the religious metaphor is also fitting given that assessing aesthetic value seems a rather mysterious process, involving the generation and maintenance of belief systems, as opposed to simply measuring objective underlying quality differences. It is how valuation occurs in spite of lack of consensus on the appropriate standards that makes literary evaluation—and literary evaluators—a rich case study for examination

Book Reviewers as Producers of Literary Value

The literary consecration process involves books moving through multiple forms of literary criticism. Literary criticism as an institution can be understood as comprising three distinct yet related branches of professional literary discourse, which collectively and successively contribute to the goal of consecrating high-quality literature.[13]

The first type of critic in the chain of consecration is *journalistic* reviewers, which is the focus of this book. Journalistic critics traditionally write reviews for daily or weekly publications (i.e., newspapers) and have the widest mandate of the three forms of criticism: to review newly published fiction. In practice, of course, journalistic reviewers are able to report on only a fraction of the hundreds of newly published books that come out each week. *Essayistic* criticism is published in more selective or specialized journals, such as monthly or quarterly literary reviews, and targets readers who have a specific interest in literature and some literary background. Rather than selecting from the entire pool of newly published works, these essayists typically select a small number of titles from those that have already received some attention from journalistic reviewers since this attention in itself conveys something about the quality or value of the novels. And finally, there is *academic* criticism. Academic criticism is reserved for scholarly publications, with primarily scholarly audiences. Focusing on specialized literary readings, academic criticism draws from an even more select group of books.

Note that I use the terms "reviewer" and "critic" interchangeably. While some may find this unpalatable, all unqualified references to reviewers and critics should be understood as referring to *journalistic reviewers* in particular. And references to other types of reviewing will be qualified with identifiers such as *academic* or *essayistic* reviewing. As one moves through these forms of criticism—from newspaper reviews, to literary essays, and finally to academic criticism—the pool of critics, the range of books discussed, and the intended audience become more specialized. And perhaps even more importantly, the artistic legitimacy of the works discussed also increases: academic criticism is conventionally seen as a pinnacle of the institution of reviewing since this level of attention has historically been associated with the canonization of authors in university syllabi and in anthologies.[14]

Missing from studies that reduce the value of book reviews to their economic consequences is the symbolic impact that reviews command. Studies sensitive to this symbolic capital that critics demand focus instead on how, for instance, reviewers construct the meaning of the books they read; that is, reading and reviewing as an act of cultural *reception*. An exemplar of this work is given by Wendy Griswold who looked at how literary critics from three separate nations had different readings of the same set of books by Barbadian writer George Lamming.[15,16] And relatedly, Corse and colleagues demonstrated how the meaning attributed to Kate Chopin's novella *The Awakening* and Zora Neale Hurston's novel *Their Eyes Were Watching God* have transformed across time. Specifically, Corse and Westervelt detail how Kate Chopin's *The Awakening* was reframed from regional tale of little importance to a uniquely American investigation of individualism.[17] Indeed, during what the authors identify as the book's period of canonization there were urgings to read the book as more than "just" feminist literature. Similarly, when Corse and Griffin studied the ascendancy of Zora Neale Hurston's novel *Their Eyes Were Watching God*, they found that the criteria used to discuss the work evolved as it became more important: initially it was poorly received and framed as a piece of regional folklore; now current framings focus on the story as a struggle for personhood.[18]

These studies are important as they demonstrate that critics do not just report on books, but also actively participate in constructing their meaning—with implications for how they subsequently are valued by readers. This occurs not only through an explicit evaluation of books, but also through the specific ways critics frame the book's topic, cultural significance, merits, and faults.[19]

The benefits of these studies notwithstanding, in this book I focus on reviewers as cultural *producers* in their own right. That is, I pay attention to the concrete steps and various considerations that go into producing a book review as it is described from the perspective of reviewers. Understanding how critics interpret and otherwise receive the meaning of books is a key part of this process, of course. But much of the extant research on reviewing is constrained to analyzing easily accessible and ready-made data in the form of published reviews. For example, empirical analyses revealing the interpretive frames and criteria reviewers employ to justify their evaluations.[20] Despite the rich insights that emerge from these data, such analyses are limited in what they can teach us about the process of reviewing, including the various decisions and considerations that shape what critics put in their reviews—and perhaps just as importantly—what they leave out.

The relative lack of scholarly attention to the *process* by which critics go about writing reviews can be understood as a result of the idea that aesthetic evaluation is (i) subjective and (ii) strategic. First, the belief that aesthetic valuation is subjective—as in random or chaotic rather than reasoned—suggests that there is little to empirically document.[21] Yet this alone does not preclude valuation from proceeding.[22] Scholars examining phenomena ranging from pricing in art galleries[23] to judging physical beauty in the modeling industry[24] have demonstrated that aesthetic valuation is not random but socially patterned—and thus amenable to study. Second, the strategic view of art and culture, owing much to the influence of Bourdieu,[25,26] suggests that aesthetic valuation is simply a tool for people to use in reproducing their own status and interests, by advancing a self-serving vision of "good literature," for example.[25] And if critics simply use reviews as an opportunity to advance their own agendas (consciously or not), then analyzing the contents of reviews is sufficient. I argue that the world of reviewing has more nuanced lessons in store for our understanding of aesthetic valuation. But excavating these insights requires us to look at work that comes before the final review is produced.

A focus on the process of reviewing enables me to attend to how reviews, including their contents and the process by which reviews come to be produced through the decision making of reviewers, bear imprints of the broader values and arrangements in which they are produced. I find that book reviews are neither simply recordings of critics' thoughts about a specific book, nor reflections of critics' self-interests; instead, reviews also include critics' general beliefs about good books, good literary citizenship, and the proper place of art in contemporary society.

My goal is to provide a phenomenological portrait of reviewing that details how critics experience and understand the process and work of being a reviewer. And by asking reviewers to reflect on the meaning and motivations behind their own evaluative practices, I am able to provide a richer account of the host of factors that affect critics' final evaluations that cannot be gleaned from published texts (reviews) alone.

In this way, this work engages the growing field of the sociology of evaluation, which interrogates how people determine the value or worth of social entities (i.e., evaluative practices), and the process by which entities acquire worth or value. A central premise of research in the sociology of evaluation and worth is that evaluation is a social practice: value is not given to us naturally, nor is it inherent in a given social entity; it is something that is mediated through social processes and the activities of social actors.[26,27] This is true of forms of valuation that appear straightforward, such as the economic pricing of goods, as well as seemingly nebulous cases of valuation, such as the evaluation of aesthetic worth.

Evaluation as a Response to Quality Uncertainty

Uncertainty has a central place in the study of evaluation. In its most general form, uncertainty is present in situations where social actors can predict neither possible future outcomes, nor the likelihood of their occurrences. *Quality* uncertainty—the challenges social actors have in determining the quality (value or worth) of a social entity—is of particular interest when studying evaluation. Indeed, one can think of the study of evaluation as the study of how individuals and institutions respond to quality uncertainty.

Economic sociologists have theorized about the different sources of quality uncertainty that confront actors. One source, the problem of *asymmetric information*,[28] broadly consists of the quality uncertainty that results from incomplete information about the object of evaluation (for instance, incomplete knowledge of the history of a used car). Another source of quality uncertainty derives from people's inability to cognitively process all the relevant information available.[29] In both situations, while the quality of goods is *knowable*, various barriers prevent individuals from accessing perfect information about the products in question.

Yet another source of quality uncertainty derives from situations where the quality of an object is *radical*. In such cases, the uncertainty surrounding an entity's quality is not due to incomplete information (as with a used car); rather, the unique properties of the entity make its quality fundamentally *not knowable* in any final sense. Karpik describes such objects as singularities. Aesthetic goods, including books, wine, art, and the like, are paradigmatic examples of singular goods.[30]

Aesthetic goods are social entities that are valued in part for their symbolic qualities rather than for any objective underlying quality differences.[31,32,33,34] Symbolic here refers to the goods' associations with particular cultural values, aesthetics, morals, and status. When it comes to assessing social entities that feature radical quality uncertainty, the question then becomes: How do we assess what is good or not in the absence of objective underlying quality differences? And how do people cope in circumstances of evaluating objects that are characterized by radical quality uncertainty?

This book provides a sociological analysis of an occupation (book reviewing) and the specific skills and practices critics employ to deal with the uncertainty of aesthetic judgment. The focus is on book reviewers' categories of experience, how they confront uncertainty in the course of their work, and the narratives they impose on explaining how they navigate uncertainty. Grounding my study of uncertainty in the lived experiences of agents of evaluation results in a phenomenologically accurate portrait of evaluating work, as well as a richer appreciation of how uncertainty and its related contingencies structure action. I speak to critics to ask them what they think they are doing, why they think they are qualified to do it, and how they make sense of their practices all at a time when the cultural ground has shifted below their feet.[35]

The empirical aim of this book is thus to specify the types of uncertainty identified by reviewers, and how these various forms of uncertainty manifest and subsequently inform how reviewers do the work of evaluation. These contextual uncertainties form the immediate context in which evaluators make sense of their actions. The focus on these different types of uncertainty also feeds into the theoretical contribution of the book. I suggest that these types of uncertainty not only structure how fiction reviewers operate, but also shape evaluation processes in other artistic and non-artistic fields as well. Therefore, these types of uncertainties can form the basis of a comparative framework for studying evaluation.

Epistemological Uncertainty

The first contextual dimension of uncertainty is epistemological. Matters of epistemology are fundamentally concerned with actions and practices aimed at understanding, processing, and producing information—including producing information about the value or worth of a social entity. The epistemological uncertainty faced in evaluative situations can be understood as operating on a spectrum ranging from low to high.

When quality uncertainty is low, we are dealing with entities whose quality is uncertain—perhaps because of the different amounts of information that buyers and sellers have—but is ultimately knowable. When quality uncertainty is high, we are dealing with entities characterized by radical quality uncertainty when value is unknowable.[36] In the case of literary works, we would say that the epistemological uncertainty faced by critics is high, as aesthetic quality is difficult to ascertain in a determinative way; such judgments often remain open ended and vulnerable to contestation. The distinction between low and high epistemic uncertainty[37] broadly relates to the distinction drawn between quality uncertainty and *radical* quality uncertainty, respectively, as discussed above.[38] Yet to fully appreciate the implications that epistemic uncertainty has for shaping evaluative practices, we need to include consideration of the technologies and procedures used to *adapt* to this uncertainty and determine quality.

What are the "appropriate" ways for coping with challenges of quality uncertainty? Answering this question involves defining what Lamont describes as "evaluative cultures," referring to the utility of identifying constraints faced by evaluators including "method of comparison, criteria, conventions (or customary rules), self-concepts, and other types of nonhuman supports" that constrain evaluation.[39] For instance, Blank contrasts two methods for producing reviews, including those based on connoisseurship and those based on repeated formal testing of products.[40] According to this scheme, the credibility of fiction reviews, and arts reviews more generally, relies on critics' connoisseurship: "the skills, knowledge, talents, or experience of a single reviewer who gives an expert opinion" based on that reviewer's "unusual talents, experience, or training."[41] Connoisseurship is an affective or experiential basis for producing valuation, unlike the evaluation of objects that appear to have more epistemic certainty, such as mechanical objects that undergo routine procedures to determine whether they do or do not work.[42] When the procedures for assessing quality are not well defined or are contested, then this can also contribute to the epistemic uncertainty perceived by evaluators.

Social Uncertainty

Social uncertainty refers to critics' inability to predict how relevant others will respond or react to their evaluations. Theoretically, social uncertainty builds on the idea of copresence: how "the presence of other actors shapes individual behavior,"[43] particularly with regard to whether we imagine others would be approving or disapproving of our behavior. Social uncertainty, as it is conceptualized here, focuses not only on how individuals imagine others will react to their evaluations, but also on what *future*[44] consequences such reactions may have for the evaluators themselves.

Social uncertainty draws our attention to how social ties inform the actual or perceived risks and opportunities for different courses of action. High or low social uncertainty is connected to the degree to which the anticipated consequences are knowable or not. When uncertainty is low, the actor has a sense of how other people will respond and thus is able to make calculable decisions about how to behave in the present.[45] When social uncertainty is high, however, there is a large range of possibilities for relevant others' to responses. This range of response is more open ended. What enables the future to be more open or closed ended is the social organization and dynamics and culture animating the reward structure evaluators themselves inhabit.

The concept of social uncertainty sensitizes us to the fact that the practice of evaluation is often done in particular contexts and for particular purposes and that the perceived or imagined reactions of others to the valence or contents of a particular evaluation may have consequences for evaluators and affect what they do in the present. The degree of social uncertainty is coupled with the nature of the reward structure in which an evaluator is operating. Specifically, evaluation may be conducted in the context of a reward structure wherein social actors may "bite back" (as we see in the case of book reviewers).

Rewards structures[46] are the social machinery by which rewards and valued resources are distributed. Reward structures vary in terms of the types of rewards distributed (such as material or symbolic), the criteria used for determining deservingness of rewards, and who gets to make these decisions.[47] How actors are concretely embedded or positioned in a field can affect their opportunities or their ability to positively or negatively respond to evaluation with their own distribution of resources. Particularly germane for our purposes is attention to the rules that motivate people to behave or constrain people from behaving in ways that will cause reward or retaliation for particular evaluations. In the case of book reviewers, book reviewing can be described as a *switch-role reward structure*, wherein authors are invited by the editors of book review pages to temporarily *switch* from their roles as *producers of books* to perform the role of *reviewer of books*—and then switch back again. (This role switching has direct implications for how critics craft their reviews, as we see in chapters 4 and 5.)

Institutional Uncertainty

Institutional uncertainty, another distinct category of uncertainty, concerns the degree of clarity and consensus regarding rules and procedures for behavior and the broader significance or meaning of the work involved in reviewing. To speak about institutional uncertainty we need to grapple with what is meant by institutions. Practically speaking, institutions are social structures, such as taken-for-granted rules, that constrain how we think and act.[48] Therefore, when referring to uncertainty of institutions we are focusing on the more or less formalized and explicit consensus about the routines, norms, organizational forms, and meanings that anchor and give coherence to reviewing as an activity.

The idea of institutional uncertainty ties into what Swidler refers to as unsettled times to describe moments of historical change when cultural schemas are in flux and therefore highly visible.[50] And things can be unsettled for many reasons, whether they be endogenous or exogenous shocks to the status quo. Book reviewing can be described as going through "unsettled times," or as experiencing high institutional uncertainty. By this I mean that as a profession and an

institution, book reviewing is undergoing transformation; and routines, meanings, and values that would ordinarily guide the practice
and consumption of reviewing are currently unstable and insecure.

In unsettled times, cultural meaning and ideologies are fore-
grounded as their existence is not taken for granted but becomes
a matter for debate and negotiation. The meaning, resources, and
understandings surrounding the practice of reviewing are "up for
grabs" as is the very idea of what a review is and what the goals of
reviews are. These types of debates or definitions are always constructed, but their fragility and negotiability are made more evident
during unsettled times or during moments of high institutional uncertainty, as there are competing ideologies and cultural models to
answer questions about how people should behave or what values are
important. How the concept of institutional uncertainty adds to the
notion of unsettled times, however, is that in the case of reviewing
as we will see, questions regarding the meaning and significance
of reviewing as a professional activity are also intrinsic to the way
reviewing is organized rather than this uncertainty being simply a
temporally bounded state.

The Study

The goal of the book is to understand how book reviewers undertake
the task of reviewing and valuing fiction, and to understand the social
factors that influence how reviewers do this work, including the epistemic, social, and institutional uncertainty they face. The analytical
focus is on reviewers' reported experiences of their roles as critics
while they were inhabiting and fulfilling their duties as critics. Specifically, I trace critics' subjective thoughts and feelings through the
review process from assignment to publication. In this way I follow
a pragmatist approach to understanding evaluation in that I follow
how critics define the different problems and tensions at different
phases of the review process and how they go about solving these
issues. I also focus on critics' statements of identity and expectations
around appropriate or inappropriate practices associated with their
role, how they go about solving some of these problems or tensions,
and how these attitudes and behaviors inform what critics put in
their final reviews.

To get at these ideas, I conducted in-depth interviews with forty
fiction reviewers who had published a review in at least one of three

influential American review outlets.[51] There is thus an elite bias in the sample of people with whom I spoke. This was intentional as I was interested in the experience of power and peril of evaluators, and how the shifting status and fortunes of traditional forms of reviewing inform how critics enact their duties. It was useful, then, to speak to reviewers and editors associated with the most traditionally significant publications in the Anglophone literary field, which have also seen some of the most precipitous losses in terms of status and resources. By doing so, I was able to capture the experiences of actors most affected by changes to the status order in reviewing. An alternative sampling strategy I could have taken would have been to include only high-status veteran reviewers for similar reasons. But I did not want to limit the study only to elite critics because this would yield only a small group of people and because I wanted to get the stories of occasional reviewers also—people who write only a few reviews every year—yet who are more representative of the field of reviewing, especially in response to the economic restructuring. A balance needed to be struck between the apparent elite-ness of my sample and how typical the stories and experiences were that I heard and report on in this study.

Yet the people I interviewed were also not entirely alike. In this group of forty, some had published reviews in the *New York Times*, the *Times Literary Supplement*, the *Los Angeles Times*, the *Washington Post*, the *Boston Globe*, the *Guardian*, and the *Globe and Mail*. While the focus of this study is on critics who write for journalistic publications such as those listed above, approximately one-half of the reviewers with whom I spoke also published literary essays in magazines such as the *New Yorker*, the *Nation*, and the *Atlantic*. And all reviewers had written about books for more than one review outlet.

The vast majority of book reviewers are hired on a freelance or single-assignment basis. Of the forty people in my sample, approximately eleven could be described as having held, at some point in time, a full-time position related to book reviewing, whether as book section editors or as columnists. It was more common that respondents made a living through other professional activities and wrote reviews on a more or less occasional basis on the side. For instance, many critics reported some combination of work as freelance journalists, creative writing teachers, academics, and—of course—authors. Of the forty, fifteen respondents worked in colleges or universities as professors. And only five people had not authored their own books. The remaining thirty-five reviewers in my sample who were authors were responsible for publishing over 160 works of fiction and nonfiction between them.

My goal was to provide a phenomenological portrait of critics' review processes, including the various social considerations and constraints that structured their understandings of what was possible. To that end, the interviews were designed to get critics to tell me their thoughts about how and why they entered into book reviewing, how they understood their role and goals as book reviewers, and their beliefs about the ethics of reviewing. I also asked them to identify reviewers they admired or disliked and what they found meritorious or offensive about these reviewers' work. And I asked critics about what qualified someone to write reviews.

When probing their specific review practices, I asked critics to reflect on recent specific reviews they had written, both positive and negative. My strategy was to ask respondents about recent and memorable review assignments, and respondents' process of completing those reviews. This helped interviewees ground their responses in concrete experiences—including various types of dilemmas and personal or professional conflicts that arose. This had the benefit of moving respondents' answers from the realm of the "honorific"[52] or highly principled self-presentation of their methods, to the realm of decision making and satisficing in the face of practical constraints. I have changed the names and work details of respondents to protect their anonymity as a condition of sharing their ideas and experiences.

Plan of the Book

The chapters that follow take the reader through the review process told from the perspective and experiences of the critics themselves. We begin with critics' initial invitation to review and follow them through the reading of the book, the writing of the review, and critics' reflections on the broader value and impact of their reviews given the precarious status of reviewing and, some could argue, reading culture at large. The book focuses on book reviewing as a world rife with uncertainty. The chapters are organized around three distinct types of uncertainty—epistemological, social, and institutional—and how the character of these distinctively infuse the reviewing process. In this way, the chapters also loosely parallel the experience of critics as they engage in reviewing and confront these different types of uncertainty throughout the reviewing process.

The first two empirical chapters explore epistemic uncertainty and tackle the question of how aesthetic quality is recognized. Chapter 2 presents the nuts and bolts of how reviewing works, including which books gets reviewed and which critic gets selected to write the review. Disabusing the reader of the idea that the "best" books get reviewed, the chapter emphasizes the practical constraints faced by editors when deciding which books deserve to be reviewed. It also addresses epistemic uncertainty surrounding who is *qualified* to review books in the absence of formal certification. But rather than answering this question philosophically, it is addressed through how reviewers come to be invited to write reviews and are paired with specific books for review.

Chapter 3 considers the challenges of evaluating books given the conventional understanding that "there is no accounting for taste." To some degree, critics agree that reviewing is utterly subjective, however, this is not to say that reviewing is utterly unreasoned or idiosyncratic. The chapter explores the procedures critics employ to determine the quality of books, including consideration of the different criteria used when they evaluate books. And we are introduced to the value of reviews as highly contextualized judgments whose contribution is required for the formation of the more generalized wisdom of the *critical consensus*.

Social uncertainty, critics' inability to predict how relevant others will respond or react to their evaluation or judgment action, is explored in the next two chapters. Specifically, in chapter 4 we see how critics confront the reality that what they put in their reviews has consequences not only for the book under review but also for the critics themselves. This is in part attributable to the switch-role reward structure, as many reviewers are themselves working writers reviewing other working writers. Throughout the chapter, I demonstrate that despite a temptation to write negative reviews of parties they may very well view as competition, critics are hesitant to be overtly negative in their reviews and choose instead to "play nice," in part driven by a blend of both sympathy for and fear of reprisal from others in the literary field. The key here is that critics imagine various implications for what they write—especially when it comes to negative reviews—and the potential (uncertainty) for retribution or causing pain informs how they behave in the present. The *reason* they have for imagining the future in the particular ways that they do is anchored in the switch-role reward structure of the reviewing apparatus.

Chapter 5 reveals how perceived *status* differences between evaluator and evaluatee condition the perceived *risks* associated with writing a negative review. Specifically, we are introduced to a double standard in the reviewing world, wherein any concerns about being openly negative in reviews disappear when the object of scrutiny is perceived as a famous or otherwise high-status novelist. This reversal of ethics is framed by reviewers as a way for correcting for perceived flaws in the way books are selected for review, especially at a time when there are fewer opportunities for books to be reviewed. By focusing on these issues, this chapter draws attention to how evaluation is driven, not only by the character of books, but also by internal logics or values within the community, including a reflexive frustration with the superstar market[53] in which critics operate.

The final two empirical chapters explore the high degree of institutional uncertainty that features in book reviewing. This refers to the lack of clarity and coherence regarding rules, procedures, and the broader meaning of book reviewing. Chapter 6 considers how the occupational structure of reviewing (increasingly a freelance activity) may be changing how reviewers understand the meaning of reviewing as a professional activity—and why critics continue to say "yes" to reviewing given all the uncertainty they encounter. It answers the question of what the place and significance of book reviewing is in the personal and professional lives of book critics as part of their professional self-concepts and projects.

In chapter 7, it is revealed how critics grapple with the question of the ongoing relevance of book reviewing given perceived tensions between its artistic and journalistic commitments. This chapter also examines how critics respond to challenges about what is distinctly valuable about journalistic reviews against the larger background of who makes up the reviewing field, including the rise of new amateur entrants and the tradition of academic criticism.

Chapter 8 concludes the book by tying together the empirical chapters to illustrate how these different types of uncertainty structure how fiction reviewers operate; here, we will consider what lessons book reviewing has for understanding the experience and enactment of power in other evaluative scenarios including other artistic fields, and non-artistic fields as well. Additionally, reflections are offered on what lessons can be taken from the multitude of stories shared by reviewers concerning how we think about the uncertain future of not only reviewing but what it means to be a reader.

Part 1

Epistemic Uncertainty

PART 1 INVESTIGATES how literary evaluation proceeds in spite of the high epistemic uncertainty faced by social actors. Evaluating works of fiction is particularly difficult because of the commonly held belief that aesthetic judgment is a matter of idiosyncratic taste, rather than objective fact. Indeed, the charge that "anyone can be a critic" emanates from this premise. Put differently, literary evaluation is a task characterized by high epistemic uncertainty because the quality of a novel is understood to be open ended: whether one argues that a book is "good" or "bad" depends on the particular criteria employed. For instance, one critic may recommend a book by Margaret Atwood as a better read than Michael Ondaatje's latest novel, or vice versa. But such valuations depend on the specific criteria or evaluative frame used to make Atwood's work and Ondaatje's work commensurable (for example, originality, authenticity, political impact, etc.), and no one criterion is universally more valued than another.

We see in the following chapters how critics grapple with their professional duty to produce reliable reviews, while also recognizing the inherent subjectivity and fallibility of their aesthetic judgments. Additionally, while the subjectivity of literary judgment is itself not a revelation, we also see how epistemic uncertainty surrounding the quality of books generates uncertainty "upstream" in the evaluation process: specifically, in terms of uncertainty surrounding who is qualified to be a reviewer and which books deserve to be reviewed in the first place. All this combines to shape how critics insert themselves as agents in the larger process of creating literary value.

Chapter 2

How Reviewing Works

IT BEGINS WITH BOOKS.

More than fifty thousand original adult fiction titles are released each year in the United States—not including self-published titles. Yet, only a small fraction of these will ever receive book reviews.[1] One book review section editor I interviewed estimated that he typically receives "somewhere in the range of 700–800 books a week" but can only cover "about 800 books a year," which equates to reviewing "about one week's worth of books in the course of a year."

Given the symbolic and economic profits to be gained from getting a book review, one might hope that the reviewing apparatus in publishing operates as an aesthetic meritocracy: that is, a system in which rewards are distributed in accordance with the merits of a book, and in which the best and most culturally deserving books are selected for review. But this is rarely the entire story of how rewards are distributed in traditional markets. Nor is it how rewards (that is, critical attention) are distributed in the world of cultural production.

This chapter attends to the selection processes and practices that affect which books get reviewed, and the related concern of how to find suitable critics to write the reviews. To address these issues, I present interviews conducted not only with reviewers but also with book review editors. It is book review editors who curate which books and voices will appear in review sections, while reviewers decide whether or not to accept review assignments and make the final judgments contained within reviews.[2] A total of thirteen people I interviewed had current or previous experience working as review editors.[3] The chapter emphasizes the practical constraints and contingencies editors face and how they respond to epistemic uncertainty surrounding their choices of which books deserve to be reviewed and what qualifies someone to be a reviewer.

The Selection of Books

When I ask book editors and critics about the primary goal of reviewing, they typically respond that they hope to direct readers toward "good books." As one book page editor noted, "There are basically too many books out there to read, and you are helping guide [readers] towards the books that are good." Another critic explained that his job as a reviewer is to tell readers why they should "give their time to this book as opposed to any of the millions of others." These responses all demonstrate an interest in steering readers toward high-quality work that the reviewers deem to be noteworthy and deserving of being read.

Selecting which books to review begins with a practice of exclusion. One editor explained that he begins with "about 150 books," and immediately his staff sorts through and whittles the number to "probably 12 books a day that we seriously consider" with the rest to be "discarded or given away." Then, once a week, each member of the editorial team "brings four or five books to a meeting. We talk about them and explain why we think they should be reviewed [and] who we think should be assigned those books." Other editors described a similar process.

Readers may be surprised that "quality" is not chief among the criteria guiding the culling process. As one fiction editor of a major daily newspaper revealed, "It would probably surprise people because we are not, for instance, looking for the best books. We haven't read the books, and we have other concerns besides quality." These "other concerns" are summarized in figure 2.1 and include a consideration largely neglected by sociologists of literature: the logistical challenges of finding "the right" reviewers.

Covering "Big Books"

When selecting titles to review, editors revealed that some books are too big to be ignored. Big books are perceived by publishers to have the best chance of becoming best sellers.[4] Whether or not a book is believed to have best-seller potential is influenced by multiple factors,

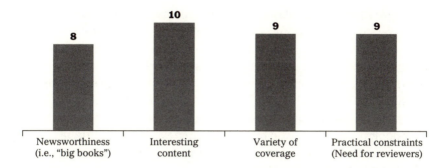

FIGURE 2.1. Criteria for selecting books for review as mentioned by book review editors. For example, eight of the thirteen book review editors interviewed mention "newsworthiness" as a criterion they consider when selecting books for review.

including the author's previous sales records, the relative success of comparable titles (or "comps"), the author's platform, and the judgments of others.[5] A consequence of a book's being perceived as a "big book" is that publishers invest disproportionate time and resources in these titles, including efforts to generate buzz and gain the attention of literary gatekeepers, such as review editors.[6]

From the perspective of review editors, the anticipation or buzz surrounding such big books makes it more likely that a book will be reviewed because of its perceived newsworthiness. One editor confirmed that "big, popular authors, when they come out with a book, most publications feel compelled to cover it." The same editor explained that he simultaneously attempts to serve two mandates with his section, "a literary kind of mandate and also a news mandate." This compulsion to cover big authors and big books is driven in part by how editors understand both the goals of their review sections and the interests of their readers.

In nonfiction publishing, newsworthy titles might include new memoirs released by prominent political figures, such as future presidential hopefuls, that are of general cultural or current affairs interest. In the case of fiction, "big novels" might include new books by famous authors. For example, one editor explained that he felt compelled to review any new book put out by Philip Roth, "not because it's a great novel, but because it's a publishing event." In other words, the "big books" get reviews because of the status of their authors; the critical attention a book receives is not, as this editor explicitly stated, because of its presumed quality but because its very publication is news in the book world.

These findings corroborate work by Janssen,[7,8] which showed that reviewers make note of the size and status of a novel's publisher, and the selection choices of other reviewing sections, in order to steer their selection practices. My interviews with critics further elucidate the thinking that is driving such behaviors. First, it is reasonable to presume that competing review outlets are guided by similar goals and constraints, which can help explain why some books—especially "big books"—get reviewed by multiple review sections. Studies elsewhere have also argued that gatekeepers may rely on status as an imperfect indicator of quality when making decisions as one way of coping with uncertainty.[9] But this is not what the editors I interviewed were saying: the above editor is explicit that he does not cover books by high-status authors (or high-status publishing houses) as proxies for *quality*, but because of a business imperative of covering books that are framed as newsworthy—even if some of these choices do not overlap or are at odds with one's "literary" mandate.

At times, the imperative to cover a variety of books, including big books, to serve the imagined interests of their readers, clashes with editors' own reading tastes. One editor explains that she strove to "make a balance between what you, yourself, are interested [in] and feel that your readers would be interested in. They cannot be at the mercy of your preoccupations." The debate of whether review sections should lead or be led by the interests of the general reading public is ongoing. One editor also reflected on the commercial requirements of reviewing: "I mean, it is a business after all. . . . We can't just ignore [readers] and imagine that these book sections would go on as little victims of our own private idiosyncratic taste." Yet he expressed frustration that "if you bring up an argument like this, you immediately get accused of pandering to readers' tastes and lowering standards and what? Do we all have to be like *USA Today*? That's just so wearisome to me." The normative role that many critics believe book review sections should play is explored more fully in chapter 7. And critics' distaste for big books and bigger authors is discussed in detail in chapter 5. But for now, it is sufficient to be aware that when a big book comes out, the decision about whether or not to review it is, as one editor referred to it, a "no brainer."

Reviewing "Interesting" Books

Just as some books are seemingly automatically selected for review, editors report excluding books they deem to be outside the scope of their review sections, such as self-published books and genres like romance.[10] Editors report that it is in the middle territory—books they could review but are not compelled to review for commercial reasons—where "fun," "creativity," and ultimately the greatest subjectivity of putting together a review section comes in. When it comes to this middle territory, the most commonly invoked criterion editors cited for including some books over others was whether the books contained interesting ideas. But what does "interesting" mean in the case of fiction?

For some editors, interesting works of fiction included books that dealt with fundamental themes and issues transcending the particularities of the story told. One editor explained that he would be interested in selecting books written by authors grappling with the big questions like "What is life all about?" Others looked for books dealing with themes like intergenerational family dynamics, memory, or investigation of a particular historical event. *Interesting* books were those that editors deemed to contain ideas of general social significance and warranting further reflection by readers.

A second criterion for interesting was also the specific way that authors approached a given topic. One editor stated that she is interested in authors who may approach well-worn topics from different angles. She would typically ask herself, "Is this [book] something we've seen a million times before?" And she applies this criterion equally to both fiction and nonfiction: "the same kind of goes for non-fiction: is this yet another installment of a kind of memoir we've seen or another book we've seen?" She loses interest if "it just feels very familiar."

Editors' emphasis on the broader social significance and novelty of "interesting" books coincides with definitions of interesting-ness in other fields. In the world of academe, Davis examines what sociological findings are viewed as interesting. He finds that sociological theories departing from prevailing expectations or assumptions are more likely to be deemed interesting.[11] Lamont examines the world of scientific peer review and finds that those research projects that take novel methodological approaches or that have broader societal impacts are more likely to be positively evaluated.[12] This overlapping valuing of novelty and social significance in the world of scientific knowledge making, on the one hand, and editors' selection of fiction, on the other, makes sense given that literary fiction is a highbrow cultural form. And part of what it means for a book to be called high-status literature is that it is not valued simply for entertainment purposes (for example, a good book to read on the beach), but is instead understood as something that challenges the reader in an intellectual way.[13] Still, editors are acutely aware that their assessments of what specific titles fulfill these criteria of interesting-ness varies.

Logistics: "We Also Have to Have Reviewers"

The final criteria informing editors' selection practices involved logistical considerations related to putting together a compelling review section. Editors' logistical considerations included space constraints (the limit of how many book reviews the section can hold); timing (books released during high-volume seasons face more competition for attention than books published during low-volume times of year); and what other books were selected for review. For example, one editor thought of his book reviews as a "collage." He aimed to select books that represented a variety of interests, but which would interact together in a meaningful way to enhance the reading experience of his imagined audience. There were also ordering effects at play: if an editor had reviewed a book that dealt with a particular theme, then the next book that dealt with a similar theme would have to cross "a much higher bar" to be reviewed. And sometimes there are just too many books to be covered: for instance, if multiple "big books" come out around the same time, then other books may be crowded out.

Having reviewers to read the books and write reviews is a crucial logistical component of putting together a review section. Many editors I spoke with had examples of times when they wanted to assign books but could not find a suitable reviewer. As one editor explained: "Sometimes, we have books that we would like to assign that we, after searching, just can't find anyone that is particularly qualified. Those books also die on the vine." The question of what makes someone "particularly qualified" to review, however, is filled with uncertainty.

Editors described finding qualified people to review nonfiction books as a relatively straightforward task. One critic, who also served as a literary editor for several years, explained that when assigning a nonfiction title, the main task is finding someone with sufficient knowledge to tackle the topic of the book: "If it's a book that's a history of Vietnam, you want someone who's a scholar of the history of the Vietnam war." The same critic contrasted this method with finding reviewers for fictional works, which is less straightforward. He explains that fiction presents unique challenges because it "has a larger emotional component than many other nonfiction works that you would assign. You want someone [who can] connect." Here, what qualifies someone to review a book is defined not by the potential reviewer having sufficient historical knowledge, for example, but by the editor anticipating which reviewers will be able to emotionally connect with the work under review.

The concept of *openness* was also highly salient to critics and review editors alike when it came to determining who was qualified to review books.[14] Openness broadly alludes to a reviewer's ability to approach a book and appreciate it. One editor emphasized the importance of reviewers who are able to "approach [a book] with an *open* mind" and guard against reading with "cultural blinders" on. Another editor explained that he is always on the lookout for someone who is "*open* to appreciating" a book. But what does it mean to be open in these ways? Why is it such an important criterion of qualification? And how does one know whether one is a good match for a particular book? Pairing a reviewer who is open to appreciating a specific book was referred as making "good match." In the next section we consider how editors and reviewers accomplished this.

Making the Match: Qualifying Books and Reviewers

As a professional ideology, the idea of a good match—pairing the right reviewer with the right book—guided editors as they chose reviewers to work on particular books. One editor explained: "I want to match [because] you get good pieces if your reviewers are positively engaged with something." Making a good match increases the chances that critics will turn in a compelling review because they are interested in the story rather than just turning in what another editor called "boilerplate stuff." In keeping with editors' concerns about serving readers' interests, not only do editors want to cover *books* that people want to read, but they also want to include *reviews* that people want to read. Editors want to publish good articles.

Regarding the fairness of the review process, both critics and editors alike invest in the ideal of the good match as a cornerstone of fair and legitimate reviewing. Although critics endeavor to transcend their idiosyncrasies as readers when rendering their judgment,[15] there is also the recognition that some people just do not like some kinds of books. And this can preclude an earnest engagement with the material under review. As one editor noted:

> We're always looking for someone who would appreciate [a] book . . . who is in a position to like this book. . . . We never want to set a book up.

We never want to send an historical novel to someone who we know hates historical fiction. We don't want to send a romantic comedy to someone that strikes us as overly serious. We're trying to match a sentiment and tone and taste with a novel.

A large part of making a good match is simply avoiding mismatches. The problem with mismatches is that they are seen as resulting in faulty reviews. When a mismatch occurs, a critic might write a negative review of a book, not because of specific qualities of the book under consideration, but because of his or her own negative prejudice toward a type of work. One longtime critic I interviewed, for example, recalled a book she reviewed that was "all about golf" and admitted: "I don't know anything about golf, and I don't care about golf!" She ended up writing a negative review of the book. She admitted that she hated the book but reflected: "I'm not sure if it's [the author's] fault or mine." What this reviewer means is that she could not be sure her negative evaluation was because of her idiosyncratic distaste for golf, or because the book was really just that bad.

Indeed, there is a concern that mismatches could result in false negatives: a negative review that is not simply the result of the quality of the book in question but also of the incompatibility of the taste of the reviewer with the book in question. The value of finding a good match is thus incumbent on both editors and reviewers equally. Just as it is important for editors to try to find the right fit for a particular book, it is also crucial that critics decide whether they are, in actuality, the right person, or a good match, for the assignment, and whether or not they should accept that assignment.

Being able to separate what is a response to the contents of the book and what is due to the subjectivity of the reviewer is especially important. The concern with finding a reviewer who is in a position to *like* a book is not seen as something that could bias the reviewer, but as a basic and first step toward finding a legitimate reviewer. This asymmetric concern with subjectivity speaks to the way novels are understood as objects of evaluation, and to reviewers' taste as a mode of evaluation. In other words, it is about working with bias in an orderly fashion.[16]

Avoiding mismatches, however, is not the same as seeking out positive reviews. What drives this search is the recognition of the capabilities and limitations of taste as an evaluative faculty, and how these predilections operate as prejudices that preclude reviewers from giving a book a fair hearing. One could argue that the critic who hated golf should not have been assigned the book on golf. And the same reviewer expressed regret that she had not simply declined the assignment since she was not in a position to appreciate the book.

If one cannot be sure whether the negative assessment is the fault of an author for writing a bad book, or the fault of a reviewer for just having a fundamental incompatibility of interests, then the evaluation itself is faulty. But avoiding mismatches is not solely the responsibility of editors who assign books: it is also the responsibility of reviewers themselves. It is incumbent on critics to recuse themselves if there is any preexisting condition that might preclude them from giving a book an unprejudiced evaluation[17] including their personal tastes.

Reviewers, for their part, similarly rely on the perception of similarities or parallels between the work under review and their own self-concepts as readers and writers to anticipate whether they will be a good fit for a before accepting a review assignment. Critics are motivated to do so to stave off any professional embarrassment that could attend reviewing a book for which they were unsuited. One critic noted that while usually the "[matching] process worked very well," he recalled a time when there was a mismatch:

> Only once did they [the editors] ask me to do something that I felt was so foreign to me, culturally, that it would be an embarrassment to have me write about. I told them so, and that they should have known better, etc. etc.

There are several reasons for declining review work. Chief among them, however, is that reviewers do not feel they can offer a fair review of the work because of the boundaries of their tastes or knowledge. Far from being exclusively altruistic, reviewers could suffer reputational damage by writing about books in spite of mismatches. For example, writing about a genre or topic about which one is unfamiliar or ignorant could lead to professional embarrassment. So while editors may initially imagine who would be an appropriate reviewer for a given title, a good match requires that the critic accept the assignment. Thus, understanding how critics perceive a good fit between themselves and books is integral for understanding the matching process.

A good match thus requires the construction and coordination of two entities: the book (object of evaluation) and the critic (the appropriate evaluator). One editor describes the matching process this way: "We try to get a sense of what that book's subject, scope, tone and quality are, [and] then, mentally (and sometimes on the internet) we go about trying to match that book" with a critic who is "in the position to judge that book, you know, in a serious appropriate way." More alchemy than formula, matching fiction titles is described by various editors as "subjective," "mysterious," and "trickier," and even as a largely "subconscious" process.

Determining what a book is "about," and the specific criteria that determine whether a critic would be a good match, then, are themselves interpretive acts of *qualification*. This involves analytically breaking down both the reviewer and the object of review into discrete qualities for the purpose of ascertaining a good match between the two. This is a highly uncertain task as there are many ways for a book to be interpreted and many perspectives a reader may bring to a book (more on this in the next chapter). This task is made even more challenging by the fact that neither editorial staff members nor critics necessarily have time to read each book in advance before determining who should read it. Some may rely on the publicity materials that accompany the review copies sent by publishers, or other tools, such as conventional genre categorizations.

Editors and reviewers alike employed homophilous logics as a way of predicting suitable matches between books and reviewers. The homophily principle refers to the idea that similarity breeds connection and that we often have a preference for entities that are similar to ourselves.[18] In the context of book reviews, similarity is used as a predictor of who might be sufficiently interested in, and appropriate for, reviewing a particular title[19]. Specifically, editors and reviewers cited similarities between the books under review, and the creative and personal life histories of potential reviewers to make a match.

Matching Based on Bibliographies

One set of qualities for making good matches involves similarities between the *content* of the book under review and the reviewer's *corpus of work*. Many critics are themselves published writers (novelists, journalists, essayists, etc.). For example, one reviewer I interviewed was also an accomplished novelist who explored sexual themes in her own books. She explained that for a long time she was the "go-to person for sex" in reviewing. She felt as though "any time there was a book with just disgusting sex in it," she'd be asked to review it. She shares the experience of a friend who had written a story featuring the death of a father and has since been asked to review what they jokingly refer to as "dead dad books." Yet another reviewer, whose first book featured an island setting, says, "I am certainly aware of the fact that, after my first novel came out, most of the books that I was asked to review were either historical or involved women on islands."

In addition to thematic matching, sometimes the perceived basis of matching was at the level of genre and form. One critic, who has published over seven books and has been nominated for multiple genre-based awards, found that he was often assigned books that he described as "skewed towards fantasy, magic realism." He was quick to point out, however, that "it's not necessarily always on my part, but having more to do with my own writing career." In other words, he does not seek out such genre assignments. Indeed, he expressed a desire to review other types of fiction but also understood why editors routinely sent him the types of books that they did: "I have a lifelong history of connection with the genre, both as a reader and a writer. I do have a certain degree of expertise." It is this expertise that makes him "suitable"—a good match—for reviewing the same.

These examples reveal that critics believe that their own identities as authors in part form the basis of their competence or qualification to review specific books. A common belief held by both editors and reviewers is that novelists bring a unique "writerly perspective" to reviewing: an intimate understanding of the creative process of writing and an aesthetic sensitivity to the craft of fiction exclusive to people who have created fiction themselves. The working hypothesis is that being a writer enhances one's ability to produce a good review, especially on a topic with which one is already familiar as a writer.

Many critics also believed that their experience as novelists enhanced their capabilities as reviewers. One critic, a novelist who has written multiple books and spoke to me while on book tour for her latest novel, explained that her reviews benefit from her perspective as a writer:

> I think that I can appreciate it when [a novel is] done very well, and I can see where—I think that I can see what's happening when it's not working well.
>
> Definitely, you know, obviously *my own work as a writer* has made that possible. (emphasis added)

This critic directly identified her experience with crafting fiction as something that has enhanced her ability to review books. Specifically, beyond simply deciding that a book is not working, she can pinpoint what aspects of a book are missing ("see what's happening when it's not working") because of her own work as a writer. This is a desirable quality in a reviewer since critics are expected to go beyond simply stating that a book is good or bad: they are expected to point to specific features of the book as evidence to support their judgment.

When one of the earlier cited book review page editors was encouraged to further explain what he saw as the advantage of a writerly approach to reviewing other writers' books, the editor suggested that "there's something about having gone through that process oneself that allows you to enter into someone else's book in a different way." He also included specific benefits:

> I think there is more a sense of process . . . more of a sense of what a writer might have been going for, whether they succeeded or not, so I think there's a little bit of a more *interior vision* of how a book works. (emphasis added)

The editor, himself a published author, believes that going through the experience of writing a book gives one access to an insider perspective on the creative process. And this is advantageous for reviewing because the critic is able to judge a book on a very nuanced level. This editor even implies that writers may have an ability to take the perspective of other writers and know their artistic intentions ("what a writer might have been going for"), which can only enhance a review. And this is advantageous when looking for a reviewer who can connect with a book.

Matching Based on Biographical Details

Another set of qualities that editors and editorial committees employ to make a match involves similarities between the book under review and the perceived *personal qualities of the reviewer*. This involves breaking down the potential reviewer into discrete biographical and personality qualities, which are then assessed in relation to the qualities already identified in books for review. Based on this assessment, reviewers are then matched with particular books according to what is perceived to be a matching of qualities. The specific qualities invoked ranged from peculiarities in reviewers' personal histories to matters of fundamental disposition. An example of the first comes from a reviewer who spent time living in Eastern Europe during the first years of a war, and who later found he was assigned a work of fiction set during the same time and place. He explained that this was a good match because he was able to "testify to the book's verisimilitude."

An example of the second—matters of fundamental disposition— comes from another reviewer who found he was often assigned what he called "misfit" books. When I ask why he thought he got matched with these misfit novels, he explained: "Well, because there are people out there who really view me as a crazy bastard!" He expresses that he has a unique quality as a critic in that he is "willing to give a book a shot in a way that other people will not," and that editors know this about him. He continued: "[Editors] know that I will probably try to understand a presumed crackpot." In this case, it is something about this critic's disposition (what he called being "a crazy bastard") that serves him with a unique quality as a critic: the ability to engage seriously and meaningfully with a book that others may write off because the content appears to be nontraditional or even erratic. He, on the other hand, was willing to look at a character and make observations or ask questions such as, "Well, maybe this guy is not such a freak," or, "If they are a freak, why are they a freak?" These examples reinforce the idea that the goal of making a good match is to harness the critic's ability to fully engage with the book under review and to write a fair and informed review. And editors and reviewers alike express that the logic and means by which critics and books are matched are good ones.

Seeking Similarity as a Skill

In many ways, the reviewer-book pairing is a variation of the person-job matching process in any other line of work, when employers seek to match candidates' skills with their own hiring needs.[20] But there is an important qualification: the qualities employed for making a good match are examples of noncertifiable skills,[21] in other words, qualifications that cannot be quantified or assessed by formal means. How does one learn whether an individual has lived in a particular foreign country during a civil war, or has a particular sensibility, or is a "crazy bastard?"

One editor likened the task of matching to being a professional therapist in terms of the types of insights one needs in order to make a good match: "Being a book review editor is an awful lot like being a shrink. I think that if you know a person's reading habits and likes and dislikes, I think you know as much about them, you know, as a trained [shrink]—you do!" This example emphasizes how ineffable the qualifications are for matching critics with books, and also what an intuitive process it is. The idiosyncratic characteristics by which novels and critics are matched present unique challenges, as these are not qualities that are easily gleaned from a CV, for example.

In response, editors, and other employers, must rely on informal methods to get this type of information, such as turning toward personal and professional networks for recommendations from peers, or relying on personal face-to-face encounters.[22,23] Specifically, editors often turn to their immediate networks since it is the least costly and most convenient way to find the people they need. For instance, when recalling how they got their first review assignments, several critics I interviewed revealed that a writer friend or professor had passed on their names to an editor without their knowledge. This was how the editors had learned of them. Sometimes an editor might become aware of a person's work or tastes by serving on a prize committee, or through chance meetings at industry events.

This was the case of one reviewer, who is also a writer. He explained that he got his first assignment at the *LA Times* when he went to an *LA Times* party in place of a friend who was unable to attend. While there, he spoke with an individual working in the review pages over cocktails and mentioned that he was interested in reviewing a book on a very specific sport. Eventually he was taken up on this offer and has since moved on to reviewing general fiction. In this example, my respondent got access to a party because of his friend. But it is significant to note that the party was also a publishing industry event, and that his friend must have been well embedded in publishing networks to have received an invitation in the first place. From the perspective of an editor looking for someone who would be a good match on a very specific topic, such informal party conversations could prove an efficient way to make such a pairing.

It is important to note that there are no formally defined criteria to demarcate who is qualified to do the work of reviewing, including no prerequisite credentials. While many critics may, in fact, have degrees in English, many do not, and none of the reviewers I interviewed indicated that an English degree was a threshold for vetting who would make a qualified critic. The situation is similar not only for arts reporters but for journalists more generally: there is no formal credentialing process for practice.[24]

Rather, selecting suitable reviewers for specific books—part of the broader selection process that determines which books will be reviewed—involves a process of qualification: the interpretive process of identifying specific qualities of both social entities to draw connections between reviewers and novels for the purpose of making a good match. A cognitive prerequisite for this matching, however, is that potential critics must be *known* to the editor in order to enter into the imagined pool of critics that editors and editorial teams will try to match to a book. And it is about being known not just in a superficial sense, but in a more specific sense. The editor needs to be aware of the types of work a potential reviewer would be open to creatively— and that is a function of personal predilection.

Getting information via networks is efficient and cost-effective. As part of the professional ideology of reviewing, the information costs of determining who would be a good match for a given book— assessing noncertifiable skills—means that editors must turn to their networks in order to gauge these types of skills. This kind of information-gathering process effectively narrows the community of potential reviewer candidates to those already embedded in the writing community. So, the reliance on tight networks to make a good match is a mechanism of closure[25] even though this may not be a conscious decision on the part of either reviewers or editors. It is a practical response to the task (making a match) that is rife with uncertainty and reliant on noncertifiable qualities, such as taste.

But even so, matching is a highly uncertain activity because simply matching based on the aforementioned characteristics does not always guarantee a good match. The task is made more diffi- cult by the fact that respondents say you cannot always foresee a mismatch. One reviewer, previously cited as successfully avoiding a mismatch, shares a time when he wasn't so fortunate when he served in an editorial capacity: recalling one reviewer-book pair- ing, he "thought that there would be a good match there because [the book's author and the reviewer] were sort of around the same similar age, similar sensibility." In spite of this, he recalled that the review was still "bad" because the author came from Los Angeles and the critic was from New York and that the latter "hooked onto a lot of clichés and stereotypes about Los Angeles and used that as a basis for the review."

The lesson to draw from the editor's experience is not that LA and New York literati should never review each other's work, but that the practice of matchmaking in fiction is filled with uncertainty. However uncertain, this is a task that editorial teams perform regularly. In this context, which reviewer will review a book is perhaps the next most consequential decision to be made in the fate of a book after the question of whether it will be reviewed at all.

Conclusion

Which books deserve to be reviewed? And who is qualified to review them? These are important questions at a time when reviewing space feels limited and the legitimacy of professional critics is being openly debated. Part of the reason these questions are tricky to answer is because of the high epistemic uncertainty confronting those engaged in reviewing: first in terms of the lack of objective quality markers for evaluating fiction (more on this in the next chapter), and secondly, the ambiguous nature of the "good match" as a professional qualification.

This chapter has revealed how difficulties in assessing aesthetic quality are partially elided by editors to the extent that finding the best or most meritorious books for review is not chief among the factors that drive editors' descriptions of how selection choices get made. Instead, what features more prominently is a range of practical constraints that influence which books get reviewed, including institutional norms of journalistic reviewing, commercial pressures, and understandings about what qualifies someone to be a reviewer of a specific title. The final review pages readers see bear the imprints of all these prior and practical considerations.

Editors and reviewers alike are conscientious about how taste is applied as an evaluative faculty through the ideal of the good match. Determining who is qualified in terms of who has the "right" taste to review a book was key to ensuring the qualification and competence of the reviewer and the fairness of the review process. Yet, the criteria on which to judge the "ideal-ness" of any given reviewer, often described as having an ability to be open to or connect with a book, are difficult to ascertain. This is especially true in the case of fiction, because the idea of what qualifies someone to review fiction is based on competencies that are highly incorporated in the individual. In the absence of formal instruments or objective criteria, critics rely on deeply incorporated criteria or ways of knowing, what Fourcade calls an embodied knowledge, that is, "knowledge that cannot be easily dissociated from the personal qualities of its bearers."[26]

One consequence of the highly personalized qualification of reviewers—in other words, taste as a noncertifiable skill—is that the practical pool of potential reviewers is necessarily limited to those people about whom editors possess this type of information. So people who are already embedded in the world of reviewing tend to be asked, not as a matter of policy, but in response to the practical epistemic challenge of how to glean information about noncertifiable qualities, such as through their bibliographies and biographical details, in order to predict fit with a book. As we see here and in future chapters, the idea that the personal is professional is salient at various points in the book-reviewing process.

Chapter 3

Accounting for Taste

ONCE CRITICS HAVE ACCEPTED A REVIEW ASSIGNMENT, their next task is to read the book and generate an assessment of its merits or failures. One critic describes his review process this way:

> I get the book in the mail. And I spend time reading it from beginning to end, scrutinizing it in that first reading, sometimes by underlining certain sections, or by putting little notes in the margin area for me to remember, bending the top corner for me to know that I want to go back to that page, and so on.
> I finish the book, and very, very often, I will need to go to the library and find other books by that author or other books about the topic. . . . After I've done that kind of research, I start doing my book review. . . . I write a first draft. I sit on it for a day or two. . . . I double check that the content and the quotes are right. . . . Then I submit it to the editor.
> A few days later, I get an edit with some questions and a request to expand or shorten certain sections. . . . Once every question has been answered, every query has been addressed, I am satisfied and the editor is satisfied, I would consider it done . . . and eventually I get a copy [of the review] in the mail, or on the internet, and a check.

The above excerpt represents a fairly typical description of critics' review processes, though there were slight variations in routines. For instance, most reviewers take some kind of notes when reading. Some critics can get to their final review in only two drafts whereas others have a far less linear writing and thinking process and thus produce closer to four drafts. Some reviewers, like the critic above, will do research on an author's oeuvre, or on books addressing similar topics, while others are content with considering only the book in front of them.

There was a great deal of overlap in critics' descriptions of what one might expect to be the individualized and idiosyncratic part of reading a book: determining whether it is any good. The Latin proverb "De gustibus non est disputandum" ("There's no arguing for taste") suggests that it is useless to argue about taste because taste is idiosyncratic, irrational, and thus inarguable.[1] And critics are well aware that readers will have wildly varying opinions of the same book and that each could be correct. As one critic acknowledged: "I feel it's very subjective. You and I could both read a book, you could think it's brilliant, I could think it's tedious and I [don't think] it's a question of right or wrong." And one longtime West Coast critic similarly reflects: "Reading is a really subjective process, and so reviewing—well, reviewing is obviously . . . subjective." But to characterize critics' reviewing practices as subjective—as in unreasoned or nonrational—is to misunderstand how critics engage with their work and how they view their task and competencies as judges.

In this chapter, we explore how critics assess the quality of the books they have accepted to review. Despite the radical quality uncertainty inherent in reviewing books, critics endeavor to produce a highly *contextualized* evaluation, specific to their own reading of a book, that may seem to have a limited value on its own, but also contributes to a larger valuing formation: the *critical consensus*.

Reading Like a Professional: Civilian and Critical Reading Strategies

> Write me a good first sentence. . . . Okay, I'm teasing a little bit, but you better write me a good first paragraph, and sure as hell better write me a good first chapter, because if you don't, I'm gone.
> —CRITIC'S RESPONSE TO QUESTION OF WHEN HE KNOWS HE LIKES A BOOK OR NOT

When I asked reviewers at what point they knew that they liked a book or that they thought a book was "working," they said it occurred to them very early on in the reading process. One reviewer reflected on a recent review assignment and said, "I think I knew within about a chapter" what the general verdict of the review would be. And for another reviewer, the judgment could come even faster: "To be honest, it can sometimes be just a few pages." Some would cite their immediate physiological and emotional, or otherwise embodied, reactions to books as the first indicator of their judgment. One reviewer explained, "When a book is good, a book is good. And I'll identify it usually in a very sort of visceral, maybe even primitive emotional manner. It just has to hit me that way."

Critics did not appear to be bothered by the apparent unintelligibility of this evaluative moment, as illustrated by the comment of one critic: "I know some people can pursue this from an intellectual perspective . . . but for me I don't think it's anything more complicated than gut reaction." Many of the critics I interviewed described recognizing a high-quality book as an unconscious process, or as an operation occuring below the surface of deliberate thought.

But critics, of course, are expected to do more than report on their gut reactions in reviews. Many reviewers state the importance of transforming their gut reactions into defensible arguments about a book's quality. And they accomplish this transformation by performing a dual reading strategy. First, critics describe engaging in a "civilian" mode of reading the books they receive. This initial reading is chiefly concerned with assessing and identifying the quality of a book as an instinctual or "gut" response to the book. Second, reviewers engage in a "critical" mode of reading, which is concerned with validating one's initial impressions through the consideration of formal aesthetic standards. As the names of these two reading strategies suggest, it is the dual nature of this process that critics perceive as distinguishing between how they approach fiction in their private reading practice and how they approach fiction when they are tasked with producing a professional assessment of the novel as critics. Below we attend to how critics characterize and employ these two forms of reading when evaluating a book.

Is This Book Any Good? The Civilian Mode of Reading

Whether or not a book makes for general good reading is one of the salient principles of book reviewing and is also reasonably assumed to be chief among the interests of the average reader. Many critics describe the first step in their review process as detaching from their professional task as reviewers and assuming the mindset of the average reader. For example, one critic explained the beginning of her process in this way:

> Well, I first try to read the book—I mean, I try to give a novel *a reader's reading*, you know? In other words, I try to just get absorbed in the novel as any reader would, whether they're a writer by profession or a doctor by profession or a plumber by profession, just somebody who likes to read stories. (emphasis added)

Indeed, many critics come to books from the perspective of someone who just likes to read, regardless of whether that reader comes from a literary or other background. These critics explain the importance of trying to read the book at least once with the eyes of someone who was not also tasked with writing a review.

This reading practice is informed by critics' attempt to anticipate the needs and interests of what one critic calls the "normal" reader, for whom they see themselves as operating as surrogates. This reviewer noted:

> The first thing I do is read it as if I'm a normal reader and try not to be picking it apart and evaluating it on the first read, because I think that really prevents a legitimate review. That's really not how anyone else is going to experience the book.

It is from this "normal" reading perspective that this critic forms "a general impression of the book, which is really just basic, did I like this, or did I not like this?" This first pass is central to how critics evaluate books.

Another reviewer explained that when he first gets a book to review, he reads it "straight through without taking too many notes, just try to read it like a civilian, you know, and go along for the ride." This "civilian" reading, or "going along for the ride," similar to the "normal reading" of the previous reviewer, thus operates as a first mode of evaluation. It is not until his next reading that he begins to make detailed notes about the book.

But sometimes, despite their best attempts, reviewers are not able to approach a book as regular readers because of poor-quality writing. One critic described a time when she started reading a book like a regular reader, but the act of reading soon became impossible because the writing itself was intrusive:

Unfortunately, when I started to read [the book], right away and literally right on the first page, I had to read a paragraph twice because things were confusing. So I was immediately out of the experience of being a reader, and I'm in the experience of being a critic, and thinking why didn't somebody edit this? That's weird, why is she using that tense? That tense doesn't even make sense.

That this reviewer was not able to just "g[o] along for the ride" as a reader is taken as an indication that something in the book was not working: she could not just attend to the story being told and ignore the mechanics of the writing.

A commonly cited indicator of good writing by reviewers was the degree to which readers were able to temporarily suspend disbelief and be drawn into the fictional world of the author. One critic articulated this principle as: "The better the book is, the more easily absorbed one is in the story." The above examples demonstrate that some critics recognize the technical accomplishment of good writing through *affective* experiences, that is, feeling engaged or absorbed in a story.

If in this first reading the goal is approaching the book as an average reader would, then the goal of the second reading is processing their initial affective responses into reasoned and intelligible arguments. To this end, critics describe employing a different mode of reading. Critics essentially treat their initial sense of whether or not they liked a book as a working hypothesis. And the function of the second more critical mode of reading is to test that hypothesis.

But Is It *Really* Good? The Critic Mode of Reading

After generating their initial impressions of whether or not they like a book, critics described going through it again, but this time with a different purpose. This second mode of reading takes into account the critics' general first impressions of whether or not they liked a book and anchors these impressions in specific observations and details about the text.

For example, one critic recalled a book he disliked because the author's voice was "irritating" but then described a moment of critical pause: "[It's] one of those things where you look at it and you go, 'Hmm, I'm having a negative reaction to this. Is it my personal idiosyncrasy or is it that this book is not very good?'" The critic formulated a hypothesis: the book "is not very good." But he must subject this hypothesis to scrutiny. Specifically, his main concern was understanding where his negative reaction was coming from: was it a function of his "personal idiosyncrasy" as a reader, or was it a function of failures intrinsic to the book? By posing the question, the critic assumed that he would be able to distinguish where his subjective preference ended and where the intrinsic qualities of the book began. In effect, these critics engage in "trials of strength"[2] that test the extent to which they are speaking on behalf of the book or on behalf of private (illegitimate) concerns—in order to base their professional judgment purely on the former.

Another example comes from the reviewer who earlier described first approaching a book as a "normal" reader. She also explained her goals with respect to subsequent readings: "If you loved it, you then go back through the book and really try to pinpoint maybe it was a particular character, or a particular portion of the story or moments. You know, what was so memorable about this book?" This pinpointing process allows reviewers to return to specific sections for use as discursive evidence to substantiate their initial impressions.

A common feature that critics pointed to as a way to substantiate their judgment about a book was its language; specifically, many critics identified the value of including direct quotations from the book into their reviews. The use of quotations allowed reviewers to illustrate particular features about a book, rather than to just make a claim; to show rather than just tell. Critics singled out James Wood, in part for his ability to use quotations effectively in his reviews. One reviewer, for example, praised Wood for "*show[ing]* us, through quotations, what he is talking about. . . . You know, categorically explaining why it was a bad book and *un-controversially proving* that it was a bad book" (emphasis added). This sense of Wood's practice as exemplary reinforces the idea that critics often aim to do more than simply report on their own personal opinions. They use the space given to them in reviews to "prove" their evaluative conclusions.

Another reviewer similarly explained: "I usually like to use quotations [in reviews] because I like to let the book speak for itself." The idea of using quotations to enable the book to "speak for itself," unmediated by the reviewer's position, allows the reviewer to treat the book as an independent ontological entity. In this regard, the use of quotations is similar to the way interpretive researchers employ quotations as evidence for processes or entities external to the analyst, such as I do in this very book.[3]

A key purpose of critics' second reading is to determine the extent to which one's reactions could be accounted for within the formal qualities of the book under review rather than by personal taste alone. Critics' reactions as readers could be transformed from purely subjective—as in private responses—into a more professional appraisal of the work to the extent that such initial gut responses could be substantiated by formal features of a book. But what are the specific criteria that reviewers employ to justify and vet their evaluations?

Evaluative Criteria

In this section, I focus on critics' evaluative criteria. I asked reviewers not to speak in the abstract about what constitutes good fiction, but to recall specific instances when they wrote favorable and unfavorable reviews, and to recall what it was about the books that they liked or disliked. I found that critics often made evaluative statements about the characters, plot/structure, language, intellectual content, and genre elements of the novels they reviewed when answering these questions.[4]

Table 3.1 summarizes the different evaluative criteria cited by critics in response to these questions. Table 3.2 summarizes the frequency with which these criteria are cited as a strength or weakness of the books under consideration.

Characters

Just under half (42 percent) of all critics interviewed mentioned the strength or weakness of characters when explaining why they gave particular books positive or negative reviews. And characters were cited as a weakness of books (57 percent) slightly more frequently than as a strength (43 percent). Typically, when reviewers were praising a novel's characters it was because the characters were rendered in a way that made them fundamentally believable or made them "come alive." One reviewer explained this quality in terms of *verisimilitude*, referring to when "an author can really drum up, you know, they can make books, the page, the writing on the page feels alive. You feel like they're describing something that really happened. There's this incredible, it's just very energetic and very honest and true and genuine."

Another reviewer expressed a similar idea when speaking about characters as part of the long list of elements she appreciated about a recent book she reviewed: "Then you have wonderful characters that

TABLE 3.1. *Evaluative Criteria Cited by Critics When Describing Good and Bad Books*

EVALUATIVE CRITERIA	NUMBER OF CRITICS (N=40)
Characterization	17 (42%)
Language or prose	31 (77%)
Plot and structure	22 (55%)
Themes and ideas	28 (70%)
Genre expectations	12 (30%)

TABLE 3.2. *Evaluative Criteria Cited as Strengths or Weaknesses of Books (%)*

EVALUATIVE CRITERIA	STRENGTH	WEAKNESS
Characterization	43	57
Language or prose	50	50
Plot and structure	38	62
Themes and ideas	52	48
Genre expectations	11	89

you're just really interested in. . . . These people are utterly engaging. They're utterly human." This belief that there was something fundamentally true about the writing was brought up regularly when it came to evaluating success of characters. In contrast, when reviewers cited characters as part of the weakness of a book, they often mentioned that the characters lacked "dimension," or were "incomplete" or "overdrawn." Overall, characterization was either praised or critiqued based on the writer's ability to achieve this quality of verisimilitude.

Plot, Story, and Structure

Plot, story, and structure are narrative elements and often refer to the formal and strategic ordering of the story. Slightly more than half (55 percent) of the critics referenced plot or structure to explain what they liked or disliked about books they reviewed. Concerns about plot and structure were more often pointed to as areas of weakness of books (62 percent) than they were as areas of strength (38 percent).

Similar to characterization, plot and structure were cited as weaknesses of a book when they interfered with critics' ability to suspend disbelief and become fully engaged in the story because of the writer's lack of technical skill. One reviewer, for example, recalled a book with a plot that "[did] not move," and about which he had negative feelings: "It has this sort of static deadness to it. It's also a poorly structured book. It dissipates to the last 100 pages. I thought it had a lot of problems that made it a very unrewarding reading experience, overall."

In contrast, good structure in a novel was taken by critics to be a mark of strength and technical skill. This could be achieved through the weaving together of multiple narratives, or the pacing of a story, for instance. One reviewer explained that part of what she admired about the book was that the author was a "genius at plotting." Likening the author's skill to a storytelling "gift," the critic said the "rollercoaster" plot "provid[es] a ride for the reader, and it has to have a loop here, and a turn there, and then flip back on itself here, and that's very conscious for [the author]." The analogy of the rollercoaster positively speaks to the reviewed author's ability to immerse the reader in the fictional landscape and to bring readers along "for the ride" through the book.

Other critics complained of plots that were "undermotivated," were difficult to follow, or were resolved in unsatisfying ways. For example, one reviewer described a book's faults as a "storyline [that] was so cheesy," and which "had every *deus ex machina* you could think of, to bail the protagonist out." Another critic was disappointed by a story line that was resolved by the power of the protagonist's capacity for positive thinking, finding it overly simplistic. Therefore, alongside concerns of not feeling immersed in a story, critics also referenced a weak plot and structure as issues that affected the originality or inventiveness of the narrative. Critics were sensitive to what they perceived as clichés, such as relationships between older men and teenage girls, or other evidence of a "dull" imagination when it came to how the book was put together.

Language

By "language" I am referring to the technicalities of writing, including how writers construct their sentences, the rhythm of their writing, and their particular word choices.[5] This was the most frequently mentioned dimension of books that critics cited when explaining what they liked or disliked about the books they reviewed. Seventy-seven percent of the reviewers I interviewed cited the language of books as contributing to their reactions. And it was equally likely that language was found to be a positive (50 percent) as it was to be found a negative (50 percent) dimension of the books under consideration.

For critics, examples of good writing were not offered unequivocally. Rather, such examples were often juxtaposed to other elements that did not work quite as well (emphasis added):

"The language is beautiful *but* the story was very hard to follow."

"Sentence-by-sentence, the book is absolutely brilliant . . . *but* overall as a novel I thought it was a failure."

"The book was very well written . . . *but* I felt that there were some problems [with] the plot and the rationale for what was happening."

Positive statements about the use of language, then, were often used as a way to soften or balance more critical comments. Technically proficient writing was thus a prerequisite for, but far from a guarantor of, a successful novel in the estimation of reviewers.

Similar to the other evaluative dimensions already discussed, what critics called "good" and "bad" language in the writing contributed to or detracted from the verisimilitude of the reading experience. When critics deemed the writing of an author to be effective, they explained that they felt there was something fundamentally real about what they were reading: they felt immersed in the fictional world created by the author. On the contrary, critics explained that they were never able to fully suspend disbelief with the work of a less skilled writer.

Sometimes this inability to become fully immersed in a book was because of the clunkiness of the language. Consider this example of clunky language given by one critic: "It was hot. It was very hot. It was very, very hot." Other times, the writing may be too labored. One reviewer explained: "I disliked this book because the author was so intrusive as a storyteller. He was performing attention-grabbing stunts with language." The reviewer explained that these "stunts" distracted from his interest in the story and in the characters because he felt "overwhelmed by this loud voice of the writer saying, 'Look at me, look what I'm doing now, and look what I'm doing now!'" In both examples, the technical efforts of the writer are too obtrusive:

the writing distracts readers and does not enable them to become immersed in (and to enjoy) the reading experience.

One reviewer described the frustrating experience of reading a book when she "really wanted to be in this world and believing it, and not outside of it seeing the puppeteer." But because of the labored writing, she could not help but see the puppeteer behind the story. She found this "disappointing," and, like the previous two examples, the intrusive quality of bad writing inhibited this reviewer's ability to become immersed in the story.

Reviewers were also critical of unoriginal writing that contained perfunctory go-to phrases. For instance, one reviewer, speaking about elements of a book she disliked, counted among them "comfortably shocking" descriptions of how "the odor of feces filled the air" when describing a murder in the book. The feeling that authors were "writing-by-numbers" was also what disappointed many critics about the books they reviewed.

Themes or Ideas

Another dimension regularly cited by reviewers related to perceived themes or ideas that were explored in the novels. The ideas contained in a book were cited by 70 percent of the reviewers; these were equally referenced as a point of praise (52 percent) or criticism (48 percent).

Critics were complimentary of books they perceived as having an "intelligence" undergirding them. One reviewer recalls a book he judged to be a success because in his estimation it "succeed[ed] very well on the surface level and on a deeper level as well." Specifically, while on the surface the book concerned the daily life of universities and families, he admired that "underneath that novel" was "deeply observant" commentary about how "so many of our institutions are untrustworthy, or collapsing or so swallowed up by other people's politics that it's just a burden to wake up in the morning and deal with that." Another reviewer praised a book for its "stunning depiction of alienation, of identity, of memory loss," and yet another reviewer was impressed by how an author treated a specific setting as a microcosm for investigating racial dynamics in America.

One reviewer took this distinction between the surface and deeper levels of a novel further. He explained that he did not appreciate a book in which he "didn't find any ideas behind the book—behind the story." He clarified: "What I'm really saying is that I prefer a book that has underlying intellectual ideas behind it that uses relationships between people to advertise those ideas." In other words, while these reviewers—and many others—appreciate fiction that tells a story, the books they deemed to be most worthy of praise simultaneously explored larger, more socially significant themes and ideas.

Sometimes, however, reviewers criticized authors because their attempt to offer a thoughtful portrait or reflection on some aspect of history or the social world was judged as a failure. One reviewer, who is an author of both fiction and nonfiction, reflected that while many of her reviews are a mix of positive and negative comments, she recalled one review she wrote of a novel that was negative for several reasons, including its representation of women:

> [The book] irritated me because I felt that it was setting itself up to be a kind of literary page-turner, almost like a literary murder mystery, and the story fell apart through the process of discovering who/why this person had done what he had done.

> Also, there were some really sort of snide and negative, or what I felt were negative depictions of women. So that was like on a personal level, I wasn't impressed with that part of the book.

And three other reviewers similarly mentioned what they saw as misogynistic undercurrents in the books they reviewed as part of the reason they disliked particular novels. It is noteworthy, then, that critics sometimes derided books that did explore ideas or topics in depth but disagreed with how some of the themes were presented. These above critics' comments also suggest another set of evaluative criteria, genre expectations.

Genre Expectations

Approximately one-third (29 percent) of critics cited the specific genre characteristics of books to explain what they liked or disliked about books they reviewed.[6] Specifically, reviewers cited genre expectation in an almost exclusively negative way (89 percent of the time) to describe why they disliked particular books.

"Genre" refers to the socially constructed categories used to group works together based on "perceived similarities"[7,8] and conventions.[9] A book's genre has implications for how the work is subsequently evaluated. Evaluative criteria or expectations are not static but are contingent on the particular frame of reference employed. For example, the following reviewer reflected on the fact that different types of fiction have their own unique evaluative criteria and contrasted them in this way:

> The literary mainstream, if you will, tends to value sort of delicacy in the handling of character, sort of an expectation that the prose will be working at a level of sophistication that you might not see in a genre book, where the genre book tends to be more dominated by concerns of plot.
>
> You know, you are trying to answer the question, if you're reviewing a thriller or something like that. Does this make me want to turn the next page? Does it achieve at creating the suspense?

What this reviewer is gesturing toward is that the complexity of characters may be legitimately sacrificed for the sake of a feeling of suspense or wanting to turn the next page, which are important factors for thriller-type novels.

I found that reviewers often cited the unsuccessful merging of elements from multiple genres as part of why they thought books were failures. One reviewer was critical of a novel that was ultimately in the thriller genre but was also flirting with elements of literary fiction. It was this genre spanning that put him off the book, which he felt attempted to "pander to the idea of literary reputation, of trying to achieve reputation within the mainstream, but it was ostentatiously done." In his own words, he ultimately "panned" the book.

Another example comes from one reviewer who was critical of a book because it set up the expectation of being a very realistic treatment but then abruptly introduced more fantastic elements. She explained: "If you write a fictional book that's taking place in, you know, modern day suburbia somewhere and you get us halfway through it before you tell us one of the characters is a vampire, you've just switched genres in the middle of it. And, you know, that's a big problem for me."

Critics' negative reactions to books that, to their minds, unsuccessfully blended elements of multiple genres is consistent with research elsewhere on the dangers of boundary spanning. Greta Hsu, for example, who observed the downside of blending genres in film, found that movies that were perceived as operating in multiple genres, such as crime and comedy simultaneously, rather than just crime, were less popular with audiences in part because the product did not adequately satisfy the expectations of either genre.[10]

Other Evaluative Criteria

In addition to the ones discussed above, there are also other frames of reference that come to bear in the evaluation of a specific title. Take, for example, what one critic described as the relative and the absolute yardsticks used to measure the work of an author:

> Let's say you're going to write about Jane Smiley, okay? Jane Smiley is a good, popular novelist. Is she great, if you put her besides Dickens and all kinds of other people? No. . . . Is she good in the context of people who are writing now? Yes. So, you say, "Do I apply the absolute yardstick, or the relative yardstick?"

Some reviewers insist on reading the writer's entire oeuvre in order to fully appreciate and evaluate the book under review if it is not the novelist's first foray into fiction. Others are comfortable taking a book on its own terms without further information about the author's previous work or about the topic of the narrative.

At times, it is not even clear if the interpretation of a novel qua fiction should operate as an evaluative frame of reference for interpreting and evaluating a book. Recalling a time when she wrote a positive review of the same book that was later savaged by a *Los Angeles Times* reviewer, one critic theorized that the differences of opinion resulted from the types of background information each brought to the book:

> I took the book on face value. I didn't do a lot of research. I didn't go back and try and find out, is this based on a real story? And I think the other reviewer did. This reviewer somehow was constantly thinking about the true story that was in the background *and making a judgment about the book on an entirely different basis.* (emphasis added)

This difference in preparation techniques is not surprising given that there are no codified rules for preparing for a review. This reviewer explained her disagreement as a function of the background knowledge she brought to her review. In other words, she "was reviewing the book as a work of fiction, a novel," rather than as a mixed genre with true-to-life historical underpinnings, which, in turn, affected the reviewers' evaluative schemas.

Reviews are not just one-to-one reports about a book and its contents, but judgment devices always provide what Karpik calls *oriented* knowledge: they *qualify* the product or book under consideration, and *orient* readers toward some characteristics over others.[12] Book critics and reviews in general do not just report on books but also frame the meaning of books in the way they choose to focus on particular dimensions of evaluation over others. And they also guide readers' attention to particular characteristics or qualities over others as well.

Yet, critics receive relatively little by way of explicit instructions or guidelines from editors about how to go about preparing for their reviews apart from word limits.[11] They therefore have a great deal of discretion and creativity when it comes to the particular qualities or criteria they bring to their evaluation of books.

Books are multidimensional. There are conventions[12] for evaluating fiction, to be sure. Considerations of characters, language, plot, structure, ideas, and genres are the common criteria that people cite when explaining what they liked or did not like about books they reviewed. But reviewers vary in how they weight these different dimensions.[13] When describing reviewing as subjective, then, critics mean to emphasize that their selection and weighting of various criteria for judging a book is itself a subjective and individual process.

The task of critics, once they have determined their final judgment about a book's quality, is to be *as specific as possible* about the specific criteria of evaluation they use to guide their judgment. This way their evaluations can be grounded and adjudicated on its own terms. One reviewer says it is the responsibility of critics "to be as clear about [their] criteria and [their] judging assumptions as [they] can be." Whether to use the "absolute" or "relative" yardstick, whether to situate a book in relation to an author's larger oeuvre or to a particular historical event, or whether to attend to language or plot—all these are decisions that critics make that actively shape how a book comes to be represented, and these decisions should be made clear in reviews. And by being so contextualized, individual reviews can be adjudicated on their own terms as well.

But what is the value of such highly specified reviews? If reviews represent the very particular reading experience of an individual critic who has made very personalized decisions about which conventional literary criteria to bring to bear on the evaluation of a book, and even then the literary evaluation rendered is still open for contest, what is the use of such a contextualized judgment?

As readers become familiar with the degree to which their literary tastes and sensibilities align with particular reviewers, readers may be able to rely on the judgments of those critics to guide their own reading choices. This is one way that a highly contextualized review can be beneficial. However, the value of highly contextualized book reviews extends well beyond this instrumental application. Specifically, these contextualized judgments and the inevitable disagreement between various reviews of the same books feed a second-order of valuation: the critical consensus.

The Critical Consensus: Productivity in Disagreement

When I asked reviewers if they could recall instances when their own opinion about a book was at odds with the opinions of fellow critics, they readily confirmed:

"Oh, sure, that happens all the time."

"Absolutely."

"Oh sure . . . there have been many times when my judgment was different from other reviewers. Many, many times."

While it is taboo for critics to consult other critics' reviews when preparing their own, it is common for critics to later read or otherwise learn about evaluative disagreements once other reviews of the same title are published. And many reviewers had several examples ready to share.

An important signal of reviewers' quality is the degree to which reviewers' judgments are corroborated by those of their peers.[14] Yet, dissenting opinions about the quality of a book are commonplace in reviewing. When asked how they made sense of these disparities, some expressed doubt and insecurity when their own opinions were contradicted by their peers.

Many critics reported feelings of professional self-doubt when they encountered reviews written by peers that conflicted with their own conclusions about a book. Often, seeing one's opinion directly contradicted could trigger a moment of professional insecurity or, as one critic described it, "a first blush of feeling, 'Oh, my gosh, did I miss something really, really important?'" Another reviewer echoed this description: "It's very nerve-racking to read someone else's review of the same book that you've read. You feel like, 'Oh, I missed that,' or, 'Gee, maybe I read that wrong.'"

Another critic described a time she was "one of the few dissenters" in contrast to the majority of reviewers who thought that the book under review was "very, very superior." She explained: "It's hard to be sort of the lonely person in the corner where there's a critical consensus [the] book is a masterpiece." This critic reiterated the professional discomfort that can come from disagreement—such as being "the *lonely* person in the corner." And when I asked her how this made her think about her own judgment, she explained: "It just makes me think sometimes I'm in step [with the critical consensus and her peers] and sometimes I'm not." Some reviewers suggested, however, that this initial feeling attenuated as one became more senior and firmly established in the literary review field.

Critics' self-doubt and concern about "missing something" or about faltering judgment relates to the high degree of epistemic uncertainty they face. Again, the quality of a book is understood to be relative, and a matter of personal taste rather than determinable fact. Critics' concerns thus relate to their efforts to uphold their reputations as careful, judicious, and "good" critics, as the following example demonstrates. One reviewer shared the story of a time he read a book and was swept away by it; he wrote a keen, positive review but later found out that many of his peers strongly disagreed about the book's worth. And after reading the criticism of his peers, he realized his mistake:

> I praised the book really highly and put it on the cover of the [book review section] . . . and the book did receive some praise, but it also received some really vicious reviews. As I read those reviews, I couldn't help but acknowledge that they [bad reviews] were right. . . .
> *I felt a little embarrassed*, and you sometimes see reference to this here and there, or *people make jokes about it.* (emphasis added)

He explained further: "It's not like everyone else hated it, but I think *more serious* critics, perhaps more judicious critics, saw the book more clearly than I did" (emphasis added). This reviewer's sense of embarrassment derived from what he saw as his own failure to be "serious" and "judicious" as is expected of critics.[15,16] And in fact other reviewers I interviewed did make jokes about him.

One of his peers, a very prominent critic, explained his bemusement after reading the other reviewer's too enthusiastic review: "I thought 'What the fuck is the matter with him? Why would he do that?' . . . I almost wrote him a letter about it" (though ultimately he did not). Part of this reviewer's reaction was due to his opinion that the offending reviewer was generally "a good critic." It does not benefit one's reputation to be used as an exemplar of the irrationality or fallibility of taste. What was even more at stake, however, was that his judgment came into question, translating into a loss of symbolic status and legitimacy (even if temporarily) among his peers. Other reviewers I interviewed cited disagreements with this particular reviewer as anecdotal evidence of the irrationality of taste and judgment.

Aside from these moments of potential embarrassment, however, reviewers were largely untroubled by dissent as a matter of principle. This is for two reasons. The first concerns the respect for the multidimensional way that people appreciate fiction, already discussed. For critics, disagreements over books arise not only from differences in taste but also from the particular combination of criteria reviewers use to judge a book. And critics understand that this process produces variation in outcomes of quality judgments.

One critic I spoke with wrote a negative review of a book that later received a "glowing review" from Michiko Kakutani, previously of the *New York Times*. How did this reviewer make sense of his difference of opinion with one of the most prominent reviewers in the United States? He explained: "It didn't make me think that Kakutani was wrong, exactly, it's just more that she appreciated other things in the book more, and she appreciated them so much more that clearly she was going to forgive things that I found very problematic in the book."

Ultimately, this reviewer emphasized how he and Kakutani focused on different dimensions of the book and gave different weight to various criteria. In this vein, reviewers can agree to disagree with others in their field because it is not that their judgment is fundamentally *wrong* but that it is based on different considerations—and no one consideration is universally valued more than others. The above critic alluded to this when talking about the weighting of criteria. In other words, not only was Kakutani appreciating different dimensions of a book, but her weighting of these different dimensions was also so different ("she appreciated them so much more") that she forgave things that the reviewer I interviewed prioritized in his own evaluation of the book.

The second reason reviewers were largely untroubled by dissent—and somewhat in tension with the aversion that many critics have to being seen as "getting a book wrong"—was that reviewers see the inevitability of critical disagreements not as something to be ameliorated but as fundamentally *productive*. That is, reviewers see the value of their individual judgments as contributing to the intersubjective wisdom of the critical consensus.

Many review outlets attempt to coordinate the release of their reviews of books to coincide with the books' publication dates. This means that several reviews of a single title are likely to be published around the same time. These and subsequent reviews of the same book would later constitute what critics refer to as the "critical consensus"—the gamut of different, individual critical opinions, including whether critics liked a book, as well as the various different reasons for liking or disliking a book. Sometimes when critics talk about differences of opinion they will talk not just about disagreements with individual critics but about disagreements in relation to the general opinion of the larger community of reviewers who are thinking and writing about the same set of novels. Thus, the term "critical consensus" actually refers to a detectable *minimal level of agreement* about a book's worth or quality.[17]

The individual reasons critics like or dislike books are of secondary importance here because reviewers speak of the critical consensus as possessing a kind of collective wisdom they assume will sift out the idiosyncrasies of individual reviewers. For instance, the following critic described the sense of relief he felt from knowing that his judgment was but "one among a multitude of voices":

I figure if I get it wrong, likely in the general mass of reviews, a consensus will emerge and will show that the book was just something that didn't appeal to [me]. The general consensus is that it's a pretty good book. I think you're insulated by the fact that yours is one among many voices commenting on the books.

The suggestion here is that the larger mass of reviews will correct, or vet out, individual errors of judgment arising from critics' idiosyncrasies as readers ("something that didn't appeal to me").

Another reviewer reflected that when she reads a book and decides to give it a good or bad review, "that's only in my opinion, and that is why it's good to have a lot of reviews to see what other people think." While critics might poke fun at or joke about individual critics with whom they have disagreements, when confronted with a conflicting judgment of a book by the majority of their peers, most reviewers yield to this collective wisdom. In this way, review(er)s are as singular as the books they are reviewing.

What critics are describing in the above comments is their place in a longer process of consecration. There is the recognition that their evaluation, manifested in their book review, is subjective, that is, highly contextualized. But as the preceding discussion shows, there is also an awareness that this is not the end of the value of the review. There is the recognition that even individual reviews contribute to the valuation of a book by the contribution of each to the critical consensus.

On one level, the critical consensus effaces the particularities of any specific highly contextualized review because it is meant to produce an aggregate evaluation of the book. But on another level, what critics' comments reveal is that the value or wisdom of the critical consensus is that it subsumes all the particularities of individual reviews and uses them to generate an overall consensus. If one review stresses the value of a book because of the weight given to characterization, and another weights its historical value more, both of those judgments are captured in the aggregate judgment of the critical consensus. Therefore, the multiple ways that a book can be evaluated—based on the specific criteria emphasized, and resulting in the particular judgment made—are represented in the critical consensus.

The critical consensus as a summary of evaluations necessarily produces a *de*contextualized evaluation of a book, but it is itself informed by and gains legitimacy by its compromise of multiple contextualized evaluations. The critical consensus by this process creates knowledge about the general quality of a book that, in relation to individual reviews, is abstracted from individual critics' experiences of the book. The critical consensus is therefore understood as more reliable or authoritative as a form of information in that it is depersonalized through aggregation.

Conclusion

Aesthetic judgment is largely accepted as a matter of personal taste; thus the quality of a piece of fiction is difficult to determine in any final sense. This quality uncertainty has implications not only for how critics approach the task of evaluating novels, but also for how they perceive the value and fallibility of their own judgments.

While the conventional wisdom may be that there is "no accounting for taste," this chapter has taken the reader through how critics do precisely so by specifying the particular criteria and contextual dimensions on which they ground their literary assessment and that are inscribed into their reviews. The result is a highly contextualized review, meaning a judgment about a book's literary worth based on the very particular selection and weighting of various evaluative standards.

This contextualized evaluation has value on its own terms. But when critics reflect on the common experience of coming across other reviews that contradict their own, they emphasize that the value of their reviews is engendered by their contribution to the critical consensus. This is understood as a "collective wisdom" informed by aggregating the subjectivity of individual reviews and transforming them into a single intersubjective valuation of a book's quality.

In discussing the critical consensus, critics are locating the place of their reviews in a longer chain of consecration. The consecration of fiction can be seen as a value chain wherein each chain represents a branch of reviewing.[18] And, as discussed in chapter 1, the artistic legitimacy of a novel is further solidified as books move from link (i.e., journalistic reviewing) to link (i.e., literary essays)—with most novels never moving past the first link at all. And the reviewers who are the subject of this book feature early on in this consecration process.

Yet, what we also see here is that critics have a distanced stance when it comes to the overall success of a book: they recognize that they are at the beginning of a longer process and mostly see their own contribution as rather diffuse. That many reviewers do not feel that their reviews have much impact in the artistic biography of an individual book or author is likely due in part to the high epistemic uncertainty inherent to aesthetic evaluation, but not exclusively so. I argue that critics' disconnection from the consecrating powers of their reviews is also due to the way book reviewing is organized as a socio-relational practice.

Part 2

Social Uncertainty

PART 2 INVESTIGATES how social uncertainty affects the ways critics craft their reviews. Again, social uncertainty refers to critics' inability to predict how relevant others will respond or react to their evaluations. Evaluations, particularly professional judgments, are typically proffered for specific purposes and specific audiences. Hence, even the judgments of evaluators are likely to be subject to evaluation by relevant others. The relevant others in the case of book reviewing are the people critics imagine will be reading their book reviews in the future.

That critics must satisfy the needs of a multivalent audience further contributes to the social uncertainty of their task. The audience for reviews includes not only the editor of a review section and the general reader of the publication in which the review features, but also other members of the literary community including the author under review. The switch-role reward structure of reviewing—that reviewers are often themselves authors invited by the editors of book review pages to temporarily switch from their roles as producers of books to perform the role of reviewer of books and back again—is crucial to understanding how critics imagine the consequences of their reviews. And how critics perceive these consequences—the range of possible reactions from their different audiences—has a distinct influence on what critics put in their reviews.

Chapter 4

Reviewing as Risky Business

It's kind of an odd bias that we have. I mean, we never ask film-makers to review our movies for us. We never ask playwrights and directors to review our plays for us. It's only in this one part of the newspaper that we go after novelists to review novels.
—EDITOR FOR PROMINENT BOOK REVIEW SECTION

MANY FICTION REVIEWERS are recruited from the ranks of people who write as part of their regular professional activities. In particular, editors expressed a preference toward recruiting people who have published their own works of fiction. For example, as one longtime editor explained: "I don't think I could put a percentage on it, but I can tell you in my mind I certainly favor novelists and writers to review fiction . . . it's a majority." A former book page editor also expressed his similar preference for findings reviewers "who review as part of their writing career [because] I'm interested in how writers approach other writers' books."

As we saw in chapter 2, editors articulated several reasons why they preferred to recruit writers to review in the first place, encapsulated by the "good match" ideal. Yet another practical reason that editors may rely on professional writers is because reviews are a form of professional writing; and editors can be reasonably sure that this pool of talent has sufficient knowledge of fiction and expertise with the written word to produce usable reviews, which as we will learn consist of articles that simultaneously inform readers about a book's content, offer incisive analysis of whether a book succeeds or not, and, ideally, are entertaining to read.

At the stage when critics are concerned with writing the reviews or preparing the reviews for publication, there is an outward shift away from their personal experience and interaction with the book toward anticipating the needs of the external audiences of the review. And their audiences are multiple. The most temporally immediate audience is the editor of the review outlet for whom the review is prepared and through whom the review must pass in order to be published. The next most proximate audience for the review is the general readership of the publication in which the review will be featured. And within this general readership is an even narrower audience of other writers and people working in the publishing industry. How critics attempt to cater to the perceived needs and interests of diverse audiences has a unique impact on their reviews.

In this chapter, we see how review editors, the imagined needs of general readers, and the unpredictability of reactions by members of the literary community influence what critics put in their reviews.

Crafting Reviews for Editors and the General Reader: The Anatomy of a Review

One of the first audiences that critics encounter is the editorial staff of the outlet for which they are preparing the review. Both editors and reviewers describe the primary goal of their reviews in terms of an intermediary function. One reviewer, also a writer of fiction and nonfiction, succinctly outlined the general goal:

> I'm also always remembering that [the review] is being read by people who are deciding whether to buy a book, or to give their time to this book as opposed to any of the millions of others they could give their time to. It's my job, in a short space, to say why I think they should or shouldn't.

In the words of one editor: "There are basically too many books out there to read, and you are helping guide people towards the books that are good. You're helping guide people towards the authors who are doing good work." What these responses have in common is the described goal of steering readers toward "good" books or book they might want to read.

In pursuit of the broader functional goal of helping readers select books from the pool of newly published fiction, critics strive to meet more specific *performance objectives,* as Shrum calls them, including *description, analysis, entertainment*, and *evaluation.*[1] It is in fulfilling these performance objectives that the influence of general reader and review editors most directly affected the crafting of reviews. Each objective requires reviewers to anticipate the needs and knowledge of their audience. And many respondents reported review editors' notes as facilitating these goals. In the next section, I discuss how both editors and reviewers understand the content and achievement of each of these objectives.

Description

The first performance objective is *description.* In order to inform readers about good books, it is imperative that book reviews contain basic information about the book under review. As the editor of one paper explained, one of the guidelines he offers reviewers is to provide the audience with a "gestalt" of the book: "You try and say, 'This is what this book feels like.'" We saw in the previous chapters that conveying what a book is like is itself an interpretive act. But a common note that reviewers reported receiving from editors regarded ensuring that the review provided sufficient information about the book (including its characters, themes, etc.) without exposing key plot points.

The descriptive objective of reviews is especially crucial in the journalistic branch of reviewing since newspapers are responsible for covering newly published fiction; and it is likely that a newspaper review will be the first encounter the average reader will have with a novel. This is unlike the types of criticism one would find in specialized magazines, for example, which are often written about books well after the original publication date.

Analysis

Despite the mandate to provide the gestalt of a book, however, critics agreed that a review should not read like a straightforward book report or plot summary. The shared value that book reviews should "have an idea" relates to the second performance objective, that book reviews contain and offer an *analysis* of the book under consideration. And editors agreed that reviews should feature some analytical depth. Apart from simply conveying descriptive information about a book and whether or not the reviewer liked it, the analytical objective of reviewing requires that reviewers have something of general interest to say about the book. And ideally, they should say it in a compelling way that would appeal to general readers.

One respondent who has worked as a reviews editor for both fiction and nonfiction titles, for example, lamented what she saw as a problem with many contemporary reviews she read:

> There's so many [reviews] that I find so disappointing because it feels like a book report. It just feels so bloodless . . . that sort of perfunctory review, full of all the same clichés—and they're not even clichés of language, but they're clichés of thought.

A reviewer had a similar complaint about what he called the "Wikipedia-model of reviewing":

> I think that there is a lazy approach to book reviewing that is modeled on a Wikipedia entry.
>
> You give a general first line or paragraph about the book where, towards the end of that line or paragraph, you are going to throw in your own opinion. Yes, this book is thrilling, or a page-turner, or poorly executed.
>
> Then, the second paragraph will be a little biographical summary about the author with information that you can get in any online encyclopedia. The third one, a little summary of the book, often using the back cover or the inside flap.
>
> Then, at the end, very quickly because you have run out of space, your view of what you liked or didn't like about the book. I think those book reviews are worthless.

Both respondents believe that reviews should contain an idea; they should not be "lazy" or full of "clichés" but should demonstrate original analytical thinking.

Critics tended to use the word "context" to refer to this imperative. As one reviewer explained: "I feel like it's the reviewer's job to say, 'Look at this book in the context of other books, and in the context of time and in the context of our world today.'" Another reviewer described the necessary summary and opinion information as mere "fluff," and strove for his review to "offer some context whereby the reader is able to understand the contribution of a particular book."

While many other reviewers also referred to the importance of providing context, the precise meaning of the term varied. Three of the most common ways context was used was to refer to: (i) the topic or theme addressed in the book (e.g., in relation to other novels that explore the dissolution of marriage); (ii) the genre (e.g., conventions of the literary thriller); or (iii) a writer's oeuvre (e.g., is it the novelist's fourth book? If so, how does it compare to previous offerings? Does it represent a great departure, or is it derivative?).

One of the ways editors helped facilitate this analytical imperative was by helping the critics balance their own specialized literary interests with the imagined interests of the general reader. For example, one reviewer, reflecting on her experience with the *New York Times*, noted that "the editors, especially, will tell you that you can't be too obscure in what you're doing in the review." Probing further:

Interviewer: Can you give me an example of what you mean by being too obscure?

Reviewer: Well, for example, if I were to take a paragraph of the book and parse the language and talk about—you know, like, "Oh, this language is beautiful because of this," and then sort of do something about iambic pentameter, like I can't really—I can't really go into the sort of craft of writing, which I think [review editors and audiences] consider to be obscure.

The reviewer goes on to observe that while it was acceptable to broadly broach the topic of rhythm in fiction, going further into the technicalities would likely be beyond the concerns of the general reader. On a similar note, an editor described the importance of ensuring that the reviews submitted to him were "not idiosyncratic, that they're not narcissistic, that they're not absorbed with their own concerns." In this way, reviewers and editors strive to anticipate and meet the interests of their readers, including offering commentary about the books that is perceptive without being too esoteric.

Entertainment

As a book review is part of a larger publication, there is a professional imperative for reviewers to write a good article. This points to the third performance objective of reviewing: *entertainment*. While the formal function of book reviews may be to inform audiences about recently published books, critics and editors alike also view the review as its own form of writing, which they want readers to enjoy.

One editor explained that a goal of his section is not only to inform readers about new books but also to provide a reading experience of value in and of itself: "We are trying to provide you with a five-minute discrete reading experience that has value on its own merit whether or not you do anything else other than read that review." What the editor is gesturing toward with the "do anything else" comment is that the success of a review is not determined by whether or not a person goes on to buy a book, for instance; this emphasizes again the idea that the commercial impact of a review is not its only, or even primary, value.

Some critics suggest that the best reviews are exceptionally well written and are the product of skilled reviewers. For example, when asked about reviewers they admired, one critic singled out Michiko Kakutani because "she writes at the same high level of prose as the writer she's writing about." Similarly, another reviewer noted that "[good reviewers] can write a beautiful review about a so-so book that ends up being incredibly informative, entertaining and better than having to read the book." In other words, the best reviewers elevate their writing in a way that can actually rival or even surpass the writing they review.

The entertainment objective of reviewing is achieved by providing the audience with a worthwhile reading experience. In this way, one can see how the book review, as its own form of writing, is a cultural object in and of itself. For this reason, this third objective—entertainment—can be reframed as reviewers working to produce original and valuable writing. Despite acknowledging the mediating function of reviews, critics and editors alike also recognize that the general reader may not be reading book reviews only for the utilitarian purpose of finding which book to read next, but also for general information about what ideas are circulating as part of a broader cultural conversation and as a form of leisure reading in and of itself (more on this in chapter 7).

Evaluation

Description, analysis, and entertainment are crucial parts to the anatomy of a review. And critics repeatedly take into consideration the needs of the general reader as a way of guiding what they should put in reviews. But reviews, ultimately, also have an evaluative function, though many reviewers take umbrage at the idea that the evaluative dimension of their reviews is about selling books.

Just as critics insisted that their reviews were more than book reports, critics, such as the following reviewer, also objected to the idea that their reviews should be viewed as consumer reports:

> Book reviewing to me is not a consumer guide. It's not "thumbs up" or "thumbs down," one star or five stars. It's not *Consumer Reports*, you know? It's not "Buy this book"!
>
> I know a lot of people do that and a lot of people want reviewing to perform that function, but I think that's a really impoverished view of what it can do.

These comments seem to clash with several sentiments presented earlier, including the ideas that a primary goal of reviewing was to "guide people towards the books that are good"; that reviewers should be sensitive to the fact that their readers are "people who are deciding whether to buy a book" or not; and that the job of a reviewer is to say "why I think they should or shouldn't" buy the book.

Reviews do contain an evaluative component; however, what critics and editors emphasize is that this is not the sole goal—and thus not the sole marker of success of a book review. As one critic expressed: "it has to be more than just a thumbs up, thumbs down on a book." She has loftier goals for her review writing:

> It has to be an interesting essay for anyone to enter whether or not they have any interest in reading that book. And whether or not you convince them to read the book they would be glad to have spent the few minutes they spent reading the review, that they would have learned something about life from having read that review *whether they went to get that book or not.* . . .
>
> It was much more of a conversation about either the subject of the book or about the ability of literature to move us or shape us or enlarge us.

Here is an explicit rejection of the idea that the worth of a review is determined by whether or not it motivates a reader to go out and buy a book. Instead, as this and other reviewers insist, reviews are meant to stand as essays in their own right in keeping with the analytical and entertainment objectives described above.

Editors can facilitate this goal by helping critics articulate and convey to readers not just that they enjoyed a book but what it was about the book that worked or did not. It is not that editors change critics' judgment about books (from positive to negative, for instance); instead, reviewers describe editors as helping them represent the book and the bases for their evaluations.[2] But editors played a role in guiding the evaluative dimensions of book reviews in another important way: critics stated that editors could affect how overt reviewers might be with criticism that is deemed to be particularly negative.

One way editors might influence critics' decision about the tone of their criticism was with regard to the editor's perceived or voiced attitude toward how openly critical one could be. For example, individual editors were identified by reviewers as being accepting of—if not encouraging—"snarky" reviews as a matter of house style. Another way is through invited input. In the case of a particularly negative book review, critics may sometimes seek editorial guidance about how (and whether) to proceed for reasons that will be discussed in the next section.

A few reviewers shared instances of *too* much intervention by editors. In particular, this was when the editor seemed to have a preconceived idea of what the evaluative tone of the review should be. At times reviewers took issue with the way that their copy had been edited, especially when it made the edited review seem more or less positive or negative than the original through changes in word choices. Reviewers viewed such actions as a grave overstepping of editorial bounds and as encroaching on their autonomy as evaluators.

One reviewer, for example, who had multiple negative experiences with a prominent review outlet, recounted a time when the editorial staff invited her to review a book but communicated that another review of the same book—also published in their pages—was not what they had hoped for: "So if one review of the book is perhaps more positive than they think it ought to be, they might say, '[That] review is really great, but we think maybe the book isn't going to be so good. I think you should take a *real critical* look at this'" (emphasis added).

The same reviewer recalled a second incident with the same review outlet, when she felt the editor was overstepping bounds. This time the reviewer was encouraged to not be too critical in her review:

I had a situation once where [the editorial staff] said, "We're sending you this book to review and, well, you know, this guy he's on the newspaper's board of directors. We don't want that to affect

how you review the book, but you know he is on our board of directors, even though we don't want this to affect how you review
this, he is on our board of directors."

I think that's a message. Don't be too rude, you know? You can
be critical, but don't go overboard.

Such experiences were reported by only a minority of critics. And
editors I spoke with emphasized that they performed minimal editorial interventions and tried to give reviewers ample leeway to craft
their reviews. Yet, it was the evaluative dimension that reviewers
were most sensitive about with regards to the intervention and input
of their editors.

I argue this sensitivity is not just about the critics' autonomy as
judges, but also about the vulnerability of their position as judges.
Critics expressed an acute awareness that the evaluative tenor of their
reviews can have implications not only for the books they review but
also for themselves as working writers. As mentioned before, there
are multiple audiences for reviews. The general reading audience is,
perhaps, the most visible of these and provides the broadest base. A
second audience—and what the above examples hint at—are those
working at the review outlet including editorial staff and even the
board of directors. But there is also a third audience—other writers—
which also affects the content of the reviews, especially when critics
are writing a negative review.

Crafting Reviews for Writers: Enter the Hornets' Nest

[Reviewing is] passionate and personal stuff happening between
writers. And so if you're going to have a career as a writer, and you
decide to be a book reviewer too, you're taking a risk.
—AUTHOR, JOURNALIST, AND REVIEWER

Writing a positive review is a relatively unproblematic task in the
sense that critics get an opportunity to read a good book and to share
with the general reader their enthusiasm for the work. Critics also
benefit from the publicity that comes from reviewing—perhaps even
currying favor with the author they praise. The perceived interests
of all parties involved are served when a review is positive: the book
under review gets positive publicity; the reviewer gains a venue to
demonstrate his or her literary acumen; and readers learn about a
new novel.

When critics find themselves having to write a negative review, however, the tensions that result from the switch-role reward structure become apparent[3]. In these situations, the tensions between different values and different interests (here engendered in the dual roles of writer and critic) become highly visible because they are brought into competition with one another and with the different values at play.

As one critic noted, "Reviewing is risky business." It is risky in the sense that the impact of critics' reviews is unknown. Most reviewers are, in effect, "critics for a day." But what they do with that day—how they convey their judgments in their reviews—can have long-term personal consequences as their work will also be reviewed in the same system. One critic described this feature of book reviewing as "an interestingly contaminated situation." Another critic explained that reviewing other novelists conjured "a whole hornets' nest of conflicting emotions."

The conflicting emotions or moral quandary, largely concerns how forthcoming and explicit critics should be in their negative assessment of the books they review, especially given that critics are aware that their reviews are being read and judged not only by the general reader, but also by a more specific audience of other people in the publishing industry—including the author being reviewed.

In its most unproblematic form, writing a negative review is simply an opportunity to be honest about the failings of a book. This operation aligns with critics' earlier comments about the mediating role of book reviewing: steering readers toward books that are good and away from the not-so-good ones. Negative reviewing also presents an opportunity to offset one's competitors. Recall from chapter 2 that making a good match between reviewers and books often involves pairing writers at the same rank, and who work in the same genre and with the same themes. In other words, people who would potentially be competing for a similar type of readership.

I find that many critics reported taking the opposite tack, choosing instead to "play nice." Several critics admitted that when faced with writing a negative review, they hedged by emphasizing how the book might appeal to other readers. One critic explained: "If I ever have to say something bad about a book . . . I kind of try to be—to *play nice about it* and say, you know, I just didn't like it, but maybe someone else might like it?" (emphasis added). I refer to this practice as "playing nice,"[4] which as a discursive practice is accomplished in multiple ways, but its overall intended effect is to downplay critics' own negative feelings toward a book and to skew the overall valence of a review in a more positive direction. This usually involved softening negative language.

In his study of theater reviewers, Shrum notes that critics tend to be more positive in their written reviews than in their vocalized comments immediately after a show.[5] There was a similar difference between critics' written reviews and their vocalization of their reviews of particular books. In an interview, one critic, for example, expressed his strong distaste for a book to which he recently gave a negative review. He concluded that the book was "a mess and all over the place!" The intensity of his criticism is noticeably muted, however, in the print version of the review, where he suggested, rather benignly, that the reader may feel a little "lost" at some points in the book.

Other ways critics played nice include filling the review with contextual details to crowd out any explicit evaluative statements about the book's overall quality or shifting the focus of the review from the merits of the particular book under review to broader criteria. For example, rather than focusing on whether the book in question is particularly strong, some reviewers said that they chose to focus on the broader oeuvre of the writer in question.

One reviewer did just this for a book that made her "furious." Despite her unequivocally negative response to the book, she revealed that she actually consulted with the editor to see if there was a way to write around her very negative judgment. She explained that she chose to "look at the author's overall career trajectory and how she's so well-known and why she's so beloved for her work" with the understanding that by contextualizing the current book within the broader context of the author's excellent prior works, it might soften the blow.

One critic described this as using "code language"—"acknowledging the competency of the book, you're acknowledging the research that went into it, or you're acknowledging the commitment the writer had. There are things that you say, you know, good job, that aren't tearing the book apart but clearly aren't glowing either." The point is that critics are hedging or muting the vehemence of their criticism when it comes to negative reviews. Critics emphasized, however, that they are not being dishonest about the absolute quality of a book—they are not writing a positive review of a very bad book—but are, instead, eliding the true intensity of their criticism.

Critics offered both benevolent and defensive justifications for why they play nice, which are summarized in table 4.1. In the next section,

TABLE 4.1. *Factors Driving Benevolent and Defensive Justifications for Playing Nice*

BENEVOLENT JUSTIFICATIONS: HARM REDUCTION	DEFENSIVE JUSTIFICATIONS: RISK MANAGEMENT
Sympathy for author at other end of the review including:	Mitigation of damage to professional ties including:
Identification with hard work and time required for writing a book	Alienation of peers, editors, publicists of author under review
Previous painful experience of receiving negative reviews	Risk of personal confrontation with author
Disposition ("I'm a nice person")	Fear of retribution in the form of:
	Negative review of own work in future
	Negative evaluations in other forums such as prize juries

I flesh out these reasons. It is worth noting here that respondents were twice as likely to cite benevolent justifications for playing nice than to cite defensive ones.

Benevolent Reasons for Playing Nice

During interviews, critics recalled instances when they wrote both positive and negative reviews of books. Recalling instances of writing unfavorable reviews, one reviewer confessed: "the thing I feel hesitant about admitting is that I will feel, kind of, guilty and depressed if I really feel I need to say something negative." This reviewer was not alone in expressing these complex feelings of guilt and trepidation when it came to writing negative reviews. It was a part of the shared experience of being a reviewer, even if some were hesitant to admit it publicly to others.

Critics remarked that one source of this hesitation came from a sense of sympathy for the writer at the other end of their negative review. For example, one reviewer expressed particularly negative feelings about writing negative reviews. When I asked her what she felt when she had to write a negative review she replied: "Oh, it stinks. It stinks." She went on to muse that her fantasy is that editors "would inherently know the best ten novels of the year and send them to [her] to review," so she would have to write only positive reviews. Part of what she feels is so unpleasant about writing negative reviews is the fact that she "know[s] that there's a human being that probably spent three to seven years working on this thing." And to be aware of the "human being" at the other end of the review is to imagine the pain that this person would likely experience at having his or her work negatively appraised. The imagined pain that could be inflicted by a negative review translated discursively into reviews that contained more plot summary, character appraisals, general discussion of genre, and other details that would crowd out any explicit statements about a book's overall quality, or that would allow the reviewer to "just hold back a little bit on really analyzing it."

The expectation of pain can emerge from witnessing that pain directly. Having written a negative review of a best-selling novelist's most recent book, the reviewer attended an event a few months later at which, coincidentally, the same novelist was one of many speakers. From the audience, she heard him quoting her review: "When he got up [to speak], he quoted my review saying, 'This was so painful.' He said, 'even after all these years of writing, even after all my good reviews, this was so painful.'" Stories of being confronted with the collateral damage of one's reviews were not uncommon.

But another main reason critics expected that the people on the other end of their review might be hurt by their criticism came from critics' firsthand experience of receiving and being hurt by negative reviews themselves. Part of the negative affect surrounding a negative review relates to the fact that many critics are themselves authors, and have had personal experience with not only writing a book, but also receiving unfavorable reviews. As one critic explained, "I know how it feels, how it felt to me to get a negative review. And I didn't want to create that for someone else." These painful experiences inform critics' behavior when they find themselves on the other side of the review in a position to inflict the same harm on another novelist.

Sometimes the shared sympathy pains of writing a book moved critics to temper their criticisms. As another reviewer stated:

> I know it from both sides of the fence. I know it from having wounded, and I know it from having been wounded. What I'd like is to call a truce and not to wound anyone.

Indeed, one editor warned that "the act of having written a book can kill you as a critic because people who have written books can sometimes be a little softer as critics because they're aware of the amount of effort that went into the production of that book." And while this editor prefers to use novelists as reviewers, he keeps an eye out for people he thinks are incapable of being critical because of their writing background.

Another striking example of how the sympathy, or shared experience of what it takes to write a book, affects how critics perceive the impact of their reviews was given by a former full-time book editor and reviewer, who recalled how his experience of reviewing changed once he went through the process of writing his own book. He began by reflecting on his experience as a book editor and how he "had a lot of novelists turn me down for reviews [because] there is just too much sympathy with the novelist" in terms of how difficult it is to write a book and see it dismissed. At first, he was amazed when he first encountered these kinds of responses from writers. But later, he reflected: "I totally understand it now." The change in perspective came from trying his own hand at writing a novel: "now I've seen from the other side," he explained, referring to the "difficulties and the agony" that are part of writing a book.

For yet others, the reason given for why some struggle with writing critical reviews is "because [s/he's] a nice person."[6] One reviewer explained that writing a negative review makes him uncomfortable with criticizing others and also "a little nervous, as I always feel when I'm writing a negative review, because I'm from the Midwest, and I'm a sort of naturally nice person." It is noteworthy, however, that while he worries about coming off as unkind or badgering, these considerations do not prevent him from writing negative reviews. It can, however, inform how those negative reviews are crafted in terms of playing nice.

The Golden Rule of Reviewing: Review as You Would Want to Be Reviewed

Recall that both critics and editors believed that the process of artistic creation equipped writer-reviewers with an artistic empathy that enriched their reviews. However, critics' artistic empathies were not limited to the creative process itself. They have in common both the labor pains involved in writing a book and the experience of getting a bad review—and this could render their other role as writers a liability. Critics' decisions about whether or not to pull their punches was informed not only by the quality of the book itself, but also their recollections of how it felt to have their books panned by reviewers and the desire to reduce the harm of such a blow. This benevolent impulse also extended to the range of considerations critics felt were appropriate for arriving at a positive or negative assessment.

For example, one critic relied on her own experience of having been at the other end of the review process to develop her own approach to reviewing. She articulated that she is guided by the question *"How would I like to be reviewed?"* This was not a hypothetical question as she was also publishing books and being reviewed. She explained: "having been increasingly reviewed myself, that taught me more about the kind of reviewer that I wanted to be."

Critics tended to cite negative experiences as some of the most instructive to their own approach to reviewing. One critic, for example, who has authored several works of fiction, explained how her personal approach to reviewing was informed by her own experience with a negative review and what she feels was an unfair reviewer. She explained that a review of her work in the *Chicago Tribune* was "very, very bad" and that she took issue with the fact that the reviewer brought in personal information about the author and consideration of the "media surrounding the book rather than the book itself" to ground the review. She found this to be "completely unprofessional." Such an experience hardened her own resolve to avoid such behavior in her own work as a reviewer: "That's why I tend to stay away from personal information." Here we see how this reviewer's personal experience as the object of an unfair review guided her own ethics and informed what she is sensitive to in her own practice when she is on the writing end of the review process.

Other sensitivities included critics who get plot points wrong because they were assumed to have read too quickly, or who did not finish reading the book that they subsequently reviewed. Critics also valued reading a book "on its own terms," in other words, reviewing the book in front of them and not the book that they wished they were reading.

These examples demonstrate how critics draw on their personal experiences of having been reviewed to inform their own professional practices when reviewing others. Specifically, they avoid practices they perceived to be unfair or otherwise inappropriate when reading reviews of their own work because they did not want to be guilty of the same sins. The *sympathy pain* many reviewers shared with reviewees is not limited to experience of facing what critics deemed to have been unfair review practices but also sensitivity to being on the receiving end of bad reviews. It is no easy labor to write a book. And it is no easier to see that labor casually dismissed. Many reviewers cited such past experiences as tempering their ability to be unabashedly honest about the degree to which they might have disliked a book.

To some extent, playing nice could be seen as acting against reviewers' self-interests. When critics are confronted with a book they feel is subpar, it makes sense for them to write a correspondingly critical review. By not writing a critical review, critics put themselves in a potentially morally compromising situation, where they (a) could be charged with being untruthful or dishonest, and (b) could have their judgment called into question (as we saw in the previous chapter with the critic who was the butt of jokes by his colleagues for praising a book that was largely disliked by the reviewing community). Additionally, such behavior can be understood as helping the competition if reviewers withhold criticism of authors who write books with similar themes or are at a similar stage of their careers. At the same time, following research on why individuals sometimes act against what appears to be their self-interest,[7] we might argue that critics choose to be benevolent because "playing nice" fulfills a substantive idea, like loyalty, as they identify with being a writer. And this identification is twofold: it occurs both in the process of writing and in the experience of getting negative reviews.

I find that another set of concerns are at play in explaining this behavior. While in the short term playing nice can appear irrational, from a long-term perspective playing nice may be completely rational, especially since what critics say today can come back to haunt them in the future.

Defensive Reasons for Playing Nice

Defensive justifications refer to when reviewers rationalized playing nice in their reviews for fear of retaliation. A bad review could have deleterious consequences not only for the novelist under review, but also for the person writing the review. Critics not only felt sympathy for the writers at the other end of the review but also experienced fear of reprisal. This is because writers remember their negative reviews. Indeed, many of the respondents I interviewed could quote directly from negative reviews they had received in the past. And the switch-role reward structure of the field means that hurts and grudges could translate into lost opportunities or other forms of unpleasantness for the reviewer.

Confronting the Collateral Damage

The world of reviewing is small: it is not unreasonable to expect that reviewers may come into contact with authors who they may have reviewed negatively. Quite literally, reviewers often come to face-to-face with the people they have reviewed because of the geographic concentration of the publishing world.[8] Several critics spoke of friends who are writers but refuse to review because they "end up going to award ceremonies, to parties, to various conferences, and they meet these people."

One critic recounted a time where she was confronted by the aftermath of a negative review she had written: "A few years later at a party, the guy's wife led this broken figure up to me and said, 'You know, you've ruined his life!'" She reflected that this was unfair: "If you can't take a bad review, you shouldn't be writing, you know? I mean, that's part of what you do is you put your book out there, and people either like it or they don't."

While she is not the only one who has had to confront the fallout from a negative review one has written, some reviewers simply tried to avoid the situation. As one reviewer explained:

> I have a number of friends who are fiction writers who, almost as a policy, do not review, either because they don't want to put themselves in a position of either making enemies of their fellow writers or feeling that they can't speak honestly about a book because the author is a friend of a friend or someone from whom they might someday need to get a job. It's such a small world.

In addition to having to face these authors, reviewers were also cautious about writing negative reviews because "it's putting your reputation and also your relationship with other writers on the line by writing negatively about a book."

The damage to one's reputation, or to personal ties with other writers, is attributable to the switch-role reward structure: the fact that many reviewers are themselves writers who are reviewing the work of their peers. The risk has to do with uncertainty—about how people who are on the receiving end of a negative review will take the criticism. This is particularly relevant given the close proximity of people in the writing community.

Another reviewer joked about worrying that the writer about whose work she wrote a negative review would be waiting for her in the bushes at her house just waiting to jump out at her. She said this in jest, but at the same time, stories about personal confrontations as a consequence of negative reviews are actually commonplace. And critics cannot be 100 percent certain about how other people will react to their negative reviews. This fear is a reality that affects many reviewers, and imagined future consequences shape how willing critics are to be openly negative in their reviews. This is why some critics prefer to "play nice": it is seen as too risky not to.

It is unclear how often such acts of retribution occur. On the one hand, two of the reviewers I interviewed shared that the authors whose books garnered negative reviews had threatened to sue them. On the other end, a handful of critics have stories of times when they wrote boldly negative reviews, expecting the receiving authors to be irate, but then receiving words of appreciation for their critical insights either in person or through emails. If individual reviewers did not have personal stories about fallout from bad reviews, the steady circulation of such stories had real effects. Incidents such as the infamous physical altercation between Norman Mailer and Gore Vidal, for example, circulate among reviewers as a kind of cautionary tale.[9] For some, this and all the other risks described above are enough to make critics think twice about how direct they should be when writing a negative review. These cautionary tales were enough to deter some people from reviewing altogether.

The Favor Returned

Another defensive reason that critics gave for playing nice came from concern that if they were brutally negative in a review, the favor would eventually be returned to them. The odds of this occurring are increased by the fact that, as we saw in previous chapters, writers who work with similar themes, topics, or forms are likely to become reviewers for one another's work, enabling potential instances of retributive reviewing.

Indeed, it is common for writers to be recruited for evaluating and giving out rewards in multiple forms in the literary field beyond reviewing. For example, there are awards for reviewing, but also fiction awards or prize juries. One reviewer noted that "giving a bad review to a fellow fiction writer is [risky]. If that fiction writer is ever on a panel, a jury for an award—they're not going to vote for your ass." The risk here is that because writers are often called on to switch to evaluator roles, if one writes a negative review, then it could create tension and professional consequences down the line.

Another example came from a reviewer who recalled writing a "pretty critical" review of a novelist whom she occasionally "ran into on the [literary] scene." And the novelist took great offence at the review. She revealed that he subsequently "posted anonymous horrible reviews on Amazon about her new novel, which she described as "that sort of classic thing."[10] She used this anecdote to explain how this experience shaped her reviewing practice, especially when it came to writing negative reviews. While she thinks that man behaved badly, she admitted, "it did make me hesitate before I'd be quite so up front in a really negative opinion." Specifically, she referred to a review she recently turned in about a book she verbally characterized as a "failure." Informed by this prior unpleasant experience, she stated: "I really actually thought this book was very bad—and that is just not going to come out in the review."

This reviewer's experience with negative Amazon reviews as the author's revenge adds another dimension to the conversation about defensive reactions. With the proliferation of web-based spaces for reviews, there are more opportunities for people to engage in such retributive reviewing practices. When it comes to traditional media review contexts, there are policies in place to minimize any retributive impulses in reviewing. Indeed, declaring and recusing oneself in the event of any conflict of interest is often among the first clauses in reviewing contracts. However, there are no such filtering mechanisms when it comes to posting reviews on places such as such as Amazon and Goodreads. For this reason, several critics remarked on the potential for such spaces to be abused by authors, friends, and family who may post negative reviews about people's books as a form of revenge. There is also the potential for the opposite too, of inflating the numbers of one's positive reviews through posting reviews via multiple anonymous accounts. For some, reader-reviewer spaces held potential for reviews free from politics *between* writers.

One reviewer explained that "all the factors that can affect a review negatively—that is to say concerns about reputation, not wanting to make enemies, wanting to get back at someone—all the sort of politics of living in the world of writers . . . plus all that is gone."[11] Critics' ambivalence toward the potential and reality of reader reviews is discussed in chapter 7.

Returning to review outlets with traditional editorial structures, review editors explained that when seeking out writers to review books for them, they did their best to weed out any preexisting relationships that might bias the reviewer. As one former book editor reflected, he tried to be mindful of what he described as "personal politics" when he assigned books:

> Every editor should ask, "Do you know this person?"
>
> It's hard not to have met someone as a writer, if you're in the literary game over time, but there's a difference between having met someone and knowing them or spending a week at their house he owned on the coast in the summer, or something.

This particular editor distinguished different degrees of familiarity between writers, especially those who are friends. He said that he had seen many times "people reviewing other people who I know damn well are friends of theirs, and I think, no fucking way should they be chosen or given the opportunity to review this book, but it happens." He reasoned, "It might be the editor's fault" for not inquiring about the relationship between writers. However, even such efforts by editors are not always successful in part because such conflicts of interest are not always easy to identify.

One reason such conflicts are not easy to identify is that a grievance or source of conflict may have occurred a long time ago, and outside the pages of the review media. This was the case of one critic who recalled a time she got a "super nasty review" of her book, which she perceived to be an act of retribution for a slight that had occurred years before during a writing workshop. She explained:

> It [the review] was just full of vinegar. And that person should never have been given my book because she was somebody who had signed up for a workshop that I was teaching at my first job, and she was being rude to the other people in the workshop, and I told her, "If you cannot be polite you're going to have to leave."
>
> And she left.

The critic interjected that even after this event she helped the ejected writer in ways that ultimately led to publishing opportunities. But still, the nastiness of the review revealed that this former workshop participant "definitely had a personal axe to grind." The idea of "axe grinding" was part of the vocabulary of norms used by reviewers to refer to overly negative reviews. And the connotation was that the reviewer was not focused on the book but was after the head of the author.

Another reason why personal conflicts may not be easy to identify is that they may not be that personal. In other words, the conflict may not necessarily be borne from personal tension, per se, but may be related to the competitiveness of the book publishing world—in a word, jealousy. One reviewer recounted stories of "friends that have gotten nasty reviews, for example, from a reviewer who was turned down by their editor, or turned down by their agent." She explained:

> So you get someone reviewing a book, and they have never met the writer. It's not like they're old high school buddies. There is no real personal connection, except they have a little axe to grind. They are coming into it [with] their ego a little bruised. . . . They're picking up the book by saying, "What's so good about this? Why did the agent take this book and not mine? Why did the editor take this book and not mine? Why did this person get this prize and not me?"

The fact that many writers are reviewing other writers puts them at risk of being evaluated on terms that extend well beyond the contents of the books that they write. And to some extent, such concerns cannot be avoided. But neither should they be courted by invoking the wrath of other writers by being overly cavalier in their criticisms of others' work. And by "playing nice," critics essentially adopt a defensive posture to the uncertainty of how people will respond to their criticism.

———

The switch-role reward structure is a unique feature in book reviewing. This situation contrasts with other cultural fields as other individuals who write reviews are *fixed*[12] in an evaluative role—they do not switch to other roles. For instance, it would be unusual to see a chef review a competitor's restaurant, or the director of a movie write reviews of other people's films. The fact that writers, as cultural producers, are asked to evaluate other cultural producers is a normal organizational feature of book reviewing, but it is not generalizable to other cultural fields.

A reviewer who is also a novelist similarly reflected:

> What other art form is there where the practitioners are also the critics? That is an extraordinarily strange thing. Film makers don't review films. Painters don't review art exhibits. So immediately there's something a little weird there. And of course, there are fewer and fewer dedicated book critics. That's more and more the way it's going to be.

There are two points to consider here. First, this reviewer's comments gesture at how notions of what constitutes a conflict of interest varies across art worlds,[13] and how the literary world is perhaps anomalous or "weird" in its permissibility. The switch-role reward structure in book reviewing is likely facilitated in part by the fact that reviews use the same form as the form of the art under review—writing. Furthermore, as we have seen, reviewers and book review editors alike may provide good reasons for why this is the case and why it may benefit the book under consideration in that it may lead to a more artistically informed review process, though the bias toward recruiting writers to review other writers also introduces other perhaps unforeseen tensions into the reviewing process as well.

A second point to pull out from the above critic's remarks concerns the decrease in "dedicated" book critics. The implication here is that as the reliance on freelance reviewers hired on a single-assignment basis increases so too does the reliance on working authors. A few reviewers I interviewed hypothesized that they would feel more emboldened to be openly negative if they had full-time reviewer positions. Yet, given editors' preferences for recruiting people who have experience writing their own novels (and therefore who have also had the experience of being reviewed) and the flexibility offered by hiring reviewers on a freelance basis, the conundrum of whether and how to "play nice" will likely continue to plague the consciences of critics and the contents of reviews.

Conclusion

Book reviewing is typically not a dialogic form. Critics do not generally get feedback from their audiences about where they may be missing the mark or providing incomplete information, and then assess and adjust their reviews as they deem appropriate. Instead, critics must *imagine* their audience, including their needs and interests, when deciding how to craft their reviews. Some reviewers describe being helped by review editors in this project, but even one editor admitted that he knows very little about the readership of his section beyond basic demographics. How critics imagine the degree of literary background knowledge and interest the general reader brings to reading their reviews is one way that audiences shape what critics put in their reviews.

We have also seen how another more specific audience has an entirely different impact on how critics write reviews. Specifically, critics face considerable social uncertainty when trying to anticipate how others in the literary community, especially the author at the other end of the review, will respond to their (negative) reviews.

In both instances, critics imagine how others will respond to their actions in the future to help justify their action in the present. Beckert refers to these as "imagined futures" or *fictional expectations*, defined as "images of some future state of the world that are cognitively accessible in the present through mental representation."[14] This is significant for how we imagine future situations to orient our decision making in the present—and these fictions are especially potent when dealing with situations of uncertainty—such as not being able to predict how people will behave or what kinds of personal and professional consequences a negative review might have for oneself down the line.

But in order for such expectations to drive action they must be coherent or appear rational. Where do these ideas of the future derive from? And from where do they derive their credibility and influence?

It is less important that such imagined futures actually occur than that they influence the present, that they resonate with people, and that they are anchored in the social circumstances in which people find themselves so that they appear legitimate. And I argue the legitimacy of the particular expectations or fictions that critics project derive in part from their experiences within the switch-role reward structures of reviewing.

In the case of playing nice as a sympathetic or benevolent gesture, critics imagine how their negative reviews will emotionally impact the writers at the other end of the review in the future. And they do this when orienting themselves to the present decision of how outwardly critical they should be when writing up a negative review. Where does this expectation come from? It is anchored in critics' own experience of having received negative reviews as fellow writers. In the case of playing nice as a defensive posture, critics imagine what potentially deleterious consequences a negative review might have on their future opportunities as writers, including the possibility of retributive reviewing. And of course, the expectation of retributive reviewing is made more coherent and plausible by the switch-role reward structure of the fiction-reviewing apparatus.

There are, of course, exceptions to the dynamics discussed above. While the majority of reviewers I interviewed express hesitation or trepidation about being openly critical in their reviews, some reviewers brought up their professional experience or identities as journalists simply reporting on the news as a way of explaining why writing a negative review did not provoke any more anxiety than writing a positive review. For yet others, writing negative reviews facilitated surprisingly positive experiences in which the potentially scorned authors actually wrote letters of thanks to the reviewer, or expressed appreciation in person when reviewer and reviewee met face-to-face. According to the accounts of these few reviewers, usually the appreciation came not for the negative review, per se, but for the reviewers' efforts to be constructive in their comments and for their sensitivity to and understanding of what the author had been attempting to accomplish with the book in question. For still other reviewers, being too positive or "gushy" in their language was something to be cautious of lest readers think the reviewers was seen as a "shill" or as unintelligent. Whether or not a reader will interpret a review to be gushy or overtly critical is still another open-ended issue.

What these examples have in common is that they speak to the degree of uncertainty that critics face when trying to anticipate the reaction that readers will have to the contents of their review. These examples also speak to how this assessment about future reactions can influence what reviewers do in the present in terms of their being cautious about how they articulate the evaluation contained in their review. As we will see, however, this level of caution and sensitivity is reserved for some writers, but not others.

Chapter 5

Aim for the Stars: Punching Up, Never Down

THERE ARE EXCEPTIONS TO ANY RULE. In the previous chapter, we saw how critics articulated an impulse to "play nice" in response to the uncertainty of how imagined others—specifically the authors on the other side of the review—might react to negative reviews. In this chapter, we continue to examine how critics consider the consequences of their reviews in terms of how they may be judged by others. But the focus here shifts to situations *wherein* the strictures of playing nice did not apply—when reviewers felt no need to pull their punches.

The criteria differentiating these two situations related to the perceived popularity and status of the author under consideration. Specifically, while the playing-nice principle was reserved for first-time and middle-status novelists, reviewers made exceptions when writing reviews of authors they perceived to be high-status writers. The exception to the playing-nice rule is best conceptualized as a double standard: *You can punch up, but never down.*

Punching up and down are relational terms that position critics "above" and "below" implied others in the literary status hierarchy. The "punch up, not down" standard, also observed in stand-up comedy, essentially implies that one can take shots at people who are higher in power than you, but not go after people with less power than you. But to whom does this apply in the case of book reviewers?

The publishing field can be described as a *superstar market*.[1] A superstar market is one in which only a small minority of individuals (the superstars) generate the majority of economic activity and concurrently receive the majority of rewards.[2] A snapshot of books released in a random month in 2007 (January) reveals that: 80 percent of books released sold fewer than one thousand copies; 13 percent sold between one thousand and ten thousand copies; 6 percent of titles sold more than ten thousand copies; and less than 1 percent of titles that were published in January 2007 sold over one hundred thousand copies.[3] This skew—that the high sales were such a small percentage of titles and that their authors account for the majority of books sold—is indicative of the superstar structure in publishing.

Most critics I spoke with considered themselves midlist writers because they had garnered some success, winning awards and publishing several books.[4] However, superstar fame continued to elude them. By implication, when critics spoke of "punching up," then, they referred to writing negative reviews of works by such superstars or brand-name authors who had achieved a great deal of success and power in the literary world. And when describing "punching down," critics were referring to writing negative reviews of newer novelists with little status.

The logic of this double standard turns on the amount of status and power that the author under review is perceived to possess. As we will see, however, the intended target is the larger superstar market of publishing more generally.

No Punching Down: Cutting New Novelists Some Slack

When it came to defining authors below them on the status hierarchy, or those they should not "punch down" at, critics often referred to first-time novelists or writers early on in their careers. And reviewers were more likely to express a benevolent stance toward these writers. Consider, for example, the comments of one reviewer—who previously ran his own review pages and had written nearly a dozen of his own books—about "cut[ting] some slack" to new novelists:

> I always cut some slack to a first-time novelist. You know, it's the first time out of the box. You're entitled to find your footing and maybe you aren't going to be as severe as you might be with a second novel, a subsequent novel or a profession you expect more from.
>
> It's an unwritten rule. If it's not, it should be. I think most of the people I knew 20–30 years ago felt the same way.

And the vast majority of reviewers I interviewed did feel the same way. Another reviewer, for example also articulated this double standard first by confirming the informal rule that critics should go easy on first-time writers: "Definitely [for] the first-time author I'm going to soften the blow."

One reason for being kinder to first-time novelists, offered by a minority of reviewers, concerned an appreciation of how authors mature as artists over time. They suggested, for example, that people "learn on the job," and therefore the standards should go up with more experience with the craft. Specifically, many mentioned that new authors were still finding their voice and learning the craft of writing; so, they deserved a break. The first novel was therefore seen as a kind of rite of passage.

Such concerns, however, seemed to dissipate as reviewers turned their attention to authors they perceived as more established. One reviewer explained that she was "inclined to be less merciful [with the work of an experienced writer] if [she] think[s] it's bad." This was because "by that time they needed to have learned a thing or two." This critic's comments cohere with the idea that first-time novelists should be cut some slack as they come to learn the craft and develop their voice as writers. But by the time authors are on to their second or third books there is an expectation of artistic growth that correlates with harsher evaluative standards. When a writer is on his or her second or third novel, or is perceived as moving up the status ladder, reviewers felt freer to be more severe in their judgment.

A frequent justification critics gave for not punching down was because they recognize that the odds of success for first-time novelists are quite slim. One reviewer's hesitance to be negative when reviewing a new writer was informed by a previous experience when she took a different tack when reviewing a book she judged to be a failure. Specifically, she said: "I never believed [the writing] for a second. It felt completely phony. It felt superficial. It felt as if I was being asked to believe something that the author had not managed to create successfully." Here we see a reference to the criterion of verisimilitude described in earlier chapters. She went on:

> [The book] was a failure. It was a bad novel, and I decided rather than being diplomatic . . . I decided to pull [no] punches, and to say just what a bad [novel it] was.
>
> And I did. And I pointed out all the reasons that I thought it was bad: poor characters, poor plotting, uninteresting language, nothing beautiful about it, nothing.

Anyway, the review ran.

I didn't know the author but I knew that she lived [on the West Coast] and there were maybe five or six letters. It was when the *LA Times* was still publishing letters in the book review, and her family, her friends, they all wrote and said how cruel I had been and how wrong I was and now insulting my review was, and now off the mark I was.

In other words, every single letter that appeared about that review took me to task and essentially said how wrong I had been.

The critic described receiving some backlash after this negative review ran in the *LA Times*. Additionally, she later learned that the review affected not only the fortunes of the particular book she reviewed but the author as well:

I also later learned that [my negative review] really affected that book and it failed, but even more than that, it affected that author. I think that in her hometown, in the major paper that her publisher lost confidence, not only in that particular book but maybe in future books.

In other words, to write that negative of a review had real repercussions. I never felt terribly that I was wrong in my critical assessment of the book . . . but it did raise for me some kind of deeper issues of responsibility as a critic.

One may observe some similarities in principle regarding the backlash this critic experienced resulting from her negative review and the stories of retribution described in the previous chapter that led reviewers to play nice. A key distinction between this case and the cases of playing nice regards the locus of the perceived repercussions. The salient repercussions are regarded as not just the angry letters written by friends and family of the reviewed author, but also the potential implications that the negative review could have on the success of the book and the writer's future career trajectory. This perception that the fortunes of newer and lower-status authors were so vulnerable to the evaluative tenor of reviews led a few critics to tell editors that they would simply not review any first novels.

Sometimes reviewers would contact editors in situations where the appearance of "punching down" would have been unavoidable because the resulting review was, by necessity, very negative. For instance, one critic recalled a time when his intense dislike for a novel made it difficult for him to continue with the review, and he called his editor to quash the assignment. He explained, "It was a debut novel, and I don't feel that you should really get out the hatchet if it's a debut novel." He further explained that his position emerged from frequent conversations with other "writers and [from] realizing what they're up against" in terms of how difficult it is to gain success and visibility in the world of writing, in part owing to the superstar structure of the publishing world. Another critic operated by the personal ethical principle that "if you are in any position of power, if you are in any position of authority, it is your obligation to help those who are just starting out."

Overall, critics described a form of noblesse oblige associated with evaluating lower-status novelists. That is, critics viewed new writers as below them on the status hierarchy and expressed the value that it was the responsibility of people with higher status or authority to act generously toward people perceived as junior or at the beginning of their careers. Or put differently, to be very critical of a first-time novelist would be an example of "punching down." In contrast to the attitudes toward first-time authors, there was little sympathy or generosity expressed when it came to reviewing writers that critics perceived as being at the top of the literary status ladder. One critic received the advice from a review editor about writing negative reviews, that "if you want to write these pure bitchy reviews, fine. But do it with somebody who has kind of earned it." This "earn[ing] it" includes not just writing a bad book but also having attained a certain level of status in the field.

Punching Up: Tanks versus Pedestrians

When it came to defining high-status authors—or those "above" them on the status hierarchy—and punching up, respondents offered vague references to authors who are "famous," or who have a "high reputation," awards, or a long-standing career (for example, "they've been writing for 25 years"). These are imprecise or incomplete operationalizations of what critics mean by high-status, as many of these critics have themselves won literary awards and have had long careers writing books.

Instead—and aside from these markers—critics tended to define who is in the upper echelons of the literary status hierarchy through a qualitative sense that these are people who are impervious to the review system. In particular, these are writers whose success was perceived to be invulnerable to negative reviews, in part because they were perceived as not needing reviews in the first place to attract readers to their work.

Many reviewers expressed the perception that high-status authors were not susceptible to the potential effect that a negative review could have on their sales, future publishing opportunities, and even emotional state. One critic pointed to the financial security of famous writers. Using Yann Martel—the author of the Man Booker Prize–winning *Life of Pi*, which was later adapted into a movie—as an example of one of the superstar or high-status writers impervious to negative reviews, the critic explained: "Yann Martel, by way of making seven figures, I mean, he's not going to be having any grief over this [a negative review], really." The mention of "seven figures" may be in reference to the report in the *New York Times*[5] that Martel received a 3-million-dollar deal to publish his third book,[6] which in the eyes of the critic made Martel indifferent to receiving a negative review; and therefore, an acceptable target for punching up.

Another critic recalled being asked to review a high-status author and similarly cited the apparent bulletproof quality of famous authors to legitimate and assuage her feelings of discomfort about writing a negative review of the work. She reflected:

> I remember being assigned a book by a very, very, very, very famous big name writer. Lots of awards, very prolific. And I hated the book. Hated it. I found myself feeling really uncomfortable—on the one hand because it was such a well-known, well-respected writer, in a way I thought, well, if I express an opinion about not liking this book *it's certainly not going to hurt this writer. It's not going to affect this writer.*
>
> In a way I felt more awkward when I was dealing with, say, a first-time novelist, or a first book for someone who I felt needed the support and encouragement. So in a way I'm surprised I felt so constrained from just flat out saying everything I didn't like about this book, but I did, because I . . . I felt like I was going up against . . . the canon, in a way.
>
> I think some people, some reviewers might have found that inspiring or exciting, to be the contrary voice. The whole thing just made me uncomfortable. I'm not being very articulate about this but the whole thing just made me uncomfortable and I think that that experience really caused me to question: Why am I doing

this? On the other hand, I still find myself uncomfortable being negative. I'm not comfortable with that either. And in a way I don't think being negative is the role of a reviewer, but I think being critical is the role of a reviewer, and it's not a role I am comfortable with.

Here the critic, who has authored several novels and award-winning nonfiction work, revealed feeling okay about not pulling any punches because of the structural position of the author under review as so successful as to be considered canonical. There was a clear status difference between the reviewer and the author under review, as the critic noted that: "This is a writer who certainly doesn't need another positive review, or certainly doesn't need any praise from me." The discomfort that this critic expressed is qualitatively different from that described when faced with writing a negative review of a first-time writer, or the types of concerns—for instance, contradicting the critical consensus—discussed in chapter 3. And more to the point, it is the status of the author and the perception that this author's fame made this author impervious to the hurt or impact of a critical review that gave this reviewer permission to proceed and be bluntly critical in her review.

We saw in the previous chapter that many of the critics I interviewed do not feel impervious to the effects of a bad review. And neither, of course, are high-status writers entirely bulletproof. One reviewer recalled a time she wrote a negative review about a famous author and reflected, "You know, I'm not a famous writer." At the time of the interview, this reviewer was "struggling" with completing her fourth book. It is noteworthy that this reviewer self-identified as "not a famous writer" as this relative positioning informed why she felt obliged to write this painful review: "I don't want to be mean to him just because he's famous, but . . . I don't want people to get away with things just because they are famous either." The notion of "getting away with" something conjures the idea that famous authors occupy a system in which they are benefiting unfairly.

It is not just the perceived status of a writer that guides the double standard articulated in this chapter; the double standard is also informed by what critics see as the imbalanced way that rewards are distributed in the literary field. One critic described the different circumstances of famous and new writers by way of a metaphor of tanks (famous, high-status writers) and pedestrians (new, lower-status writers):

> Richard Ford has suggested that if you write a bad review that it's the equivalent of running over a pedestrian with a car. I don't entirely agree with that because I think some people have really—they're driving armored tanks. . . .
>
> If you have reached a point where you've been celebrated [then] it's totally open season, as far as I'm concerned.

While this critic is referring to a double standard in terms of whose books are fair game for no-holds-barred negative reviews (the tanks) and whose are not (the pedestrians), reviewers' different treatment of higher- and lower-status writers is not just attributable to a difference of success. It is also a commentary on the skewed reward system in publishing and how different people face different odds and vulnerabilities as a result.

"Pedestrian[s]" and "armored tanks" are metaphors for the different circumstances faced by authors in the "superstar structure" of the publishing field.[7] But beyond the fact that some authors are more or less successful than others, in the next section we see how punching up is understood as a critique of, if not a corrective to, the process by which such success and status are maintained.

Punching Up as Protest

The book-publishing market is a superstar market. And the reviewing apparatus plays a part in this superstar structure in that one form of reward that is disproportionately concentrated among famous or high-status writers is critical attention in the form of reviews.

Status advantage refers to when high-status people are "rewarded disproportionately to the quality of their performance" or are the beneficiaries of "outcomes from resource-allocation decisions where higher-status actors earn an allocation that is disproportionate to their relative quality."[8,9] Applied to the case of book reviewing, the attention of critics is an important resource unequally distributed across books and authors. And many reviewers were critical of what they viewed to be the unfair distribution of review attention allotted to superstar authors based not on the merits of individual books but factors that amount to status advantage processes.

Specifically, status advantage in book reviewing was described as manifesting in two ways. One is in terms of the fact of getting *review coverage*; the second is about the perceived (and suspicious) automatic celebration of famous authors—in other words, their *unde-*

served praise. Both informed critics' explanations for why they felt it was reasonable to be harsher with high-status writers.

Coverage: Stephen King Doesn't Need Another Book Review

The first way that status advantage is made manifest is in the *coverage* and publicity that high-status authors receive. A common justification given for the legitimacy and acceptable practice of punching up is a dissatisfaction with the nature of the superstar structure in publishing wherein most of the rewards go to those select few at the top of publishing world. These rewards include increasingly scarce and therefore more valuable book review real estate. More specifically, critics expressed frustration that famous authors get reviewed even though they really do not need the visibility or publicity.

Stephen King was the most frequently cited example of a famous author being needlessly reviewed: it was perceived by reviewers as needless because authors of Stephen King's status and popularity have built-in readers who will learn about and buy his books whether or not they receive review coverage and no matter what that reviewer has to say about the quality of the work. Reviewing famous authors was framed as a zero-sum game: as one reviewer explained, when Stephen King gets a review "an unknown writer, or a new writer [who] *needs* it" (emphasis added) does not get coverage. Critics' annoyance that famous authors who do not need additional exposure continue to be reviewed is related to the recognition that there are many other new and deserving writers who are writing books each year to little critical attention. This exacerbates feelings of guilt, especially regarding first-time writers; therefore, the impulse to punch up but not down can be seen as two sides of the same coin.

Critics' observations are not unfounded. As we saw in chapter 2, editors described the need to cover "big books." As one editor explained, his selection criteria were informed by more than the quality of the books he received: there was also a news imperative. In other words, review page editors chose books to review was not just by deciding which were the best books: there was also the need to cover books considered newsworthy because of the fame or status of the author involved. In this way, some authors—especially famous ones—become unavoidable figures in review pages.

In response, some reviewers offered that if precious review space is being given to famous authors, then these books should be taken to task. For example, one critic lamented that "there are fewer and fewer reviews published" today, but he recognized that there are some books that *have* to be reviewed. Against this background, he reasoned that the responsible thing for him to do was to use whatever review space was available to him to "draw attention to worthy work" on the one hand, and to "call attention to work that is dishonest or exploitive or second rate—but *unavoidable*" (emphasis added) on the other. The idea of *unavoidable* books refers to the tendency to review big books and brand-name writers.

This reviewer reflected on the fact that as there are so few reviews written today, it is regrettable that so much attention is given to people who do not necessarily need it. Yet, having their books reviewed is "unavoidable" because of their superstar status. Given that so few books get reviewed, he would prefer to use reviews to draw attention to books that people should read rather than write negative reviews about books that, in his judgment, do not have merit. Indeed, the same reviewer explained: "for most authors, if the book is just not good I'd just as soon let it pass in silence. It would hardly be the only book that's passed over [laughter]."

Though critics lament that superstar authors always receive review coverage and reviewers themselves do not have decision-making power to select books for review, some reviewers do focus on their control over how the books they are assigned will be treated in those reviews. The same reviewer, above, reasoned that if editors are intent on using valuable review space to cover "event" books, then he would use it to draw attention to famous novelists producing subpar work.

Undeserved Praise: The Emperor Is Wearing No Clothes

A second way critics saw status advantage accruing was in the perceived overpraising of books written by famous writers, in other words, when the status of the author effectively extended a halo effect on the evaluation of the book itself.

One critic framed his practice of punching up as a matter of moral fortitude. He shared an example of a time he wrote a negative review of an author who he described as "wildly over-praised" and revealed that "there's like an 'Emperor's New Clothes' kind of feeling, like you're going to be the little boy that points out that this is actually not so good."[10] The above critic referenced this story to contextualize his own critical reviews of famous people who had perhaps become so popular that few people were willing to criticize their work.

There is evidence that sometimes status influences the evaluation of books. Take, for example, the anecdotal experiences of high-status writers who publish books under a pseudonym so that their previous fame or status does not trail them. One famous example comes from J. K. Rowling, the author of the Harry Potter series, who published a book in the crime thriller genre under the name Robert Galbraith. Rowling's first "adult" novel after the Harry Potter series, penned under her own name, was received negatively, especially under the shadow of her past success. But when she published under the pseudonym Robert Galbraith, her book was received by reviewers more generously. This pattern could be understood as the result of Rowling's fame and status as a superstar writer resulting in reviewers punching up in the case of the first book, and perhaps even the stricture against punching down in the case of the novel of "Galbraith," who was a fictitious new talent.

The idea of punching up as a corrective to the influence of superstar status in reviewing was shared by another reviewer who was cognizant that he had gained a reputation for writing very critical reviews of authors. As with other reviewers profiled in this chapter, he immediately justified the intensity of his criticisms by pointing to the status of the authors about whom he wrote: "All of those negative reviews were reviews of established authors, and in those cases I feel like it's important—without being a jerk about it—it's important to be responsible and say, 'This one isn't so good.'"

Critics' feelings of being free to punch up but not punch down is given justification in the perceived flaws in the distribution of rewards in publishing, especially the status advantages accrued in fiction writing and its superstar market. In this way, critics see the reviewing apparatus as directly implicated in the imbalanced reward structure of publishing. With the evaluation of high-status authors viewed with an attitude of suspicion about whether the review attention is deserved in the first place, reviewers are perhaps more likely to be openly critical about the work of high-status people in conscious correction of or defense against what some see as an influence of status—in other words, of famous people "getting a pass."

The willingness to be nakedly critical of famous writers is in part enabled by the understanding that even if critics review books negatively, famous authors are going to continue to find readers, and they are likely still going to get another book contract and the opportunity to publish again. Therefore, in this structure, critics feel that the superstars do not have to be praised, and there is no assumption that it is going to be a good book just because they are famous or enjoy high status. And given that the entire structure is skewed toward these high-status individuals, the reviewing juncture is one point at which individual critics, who are also writers, are able to intervene in the larger machinery by which praise and rewards are distributed—at least by way of negative reviews.

For all this moralizing justification, another explanation for punching up could be a simple matter of envy, that is, less successful authors projecting their frustrations onto high-status authors. While such dynamics may also be in play, studies suggest that the propensity to be less generous when evaluating or judging high-status individuals is a more general phenomenon not restricted to low-status individuals, but also used by fellow high-status others.[11] In other words, even high-status actors, such as other brand-name authors, are less likely to be generous in evaluating fellow brand-name writers. Yet, as we will see below, reserving harsh words for brand-name authors may actually be having the opposite of the intended effect on the superstar structure of the book world.

The Conservative Effect

Critics were most comfortable being vocal about their dislike of books written by famous novelists. And this relative ease is driven, in part, by critics' recognition and frustration with the superstar[12] dynamics in publishing, which concentrates the majority of awards, sales, and other resources—including review attention—among a small number of authors at the very top of the status hierarchy.

But here is the peculiar paradox of their situation: critics express greater boldness and freedom to exercise their power as reviewers in situations where their judgments do not matter. This can be seen in the justifications for punching up, including the belief that big writers were not impacted in terms of losing sleep or shedding tears over bad reviews; and more significantly, that these types of authors will find another book deal opportunity, be granted another review, and find more readers regardless of what the reviewer wrote.

There appears to be an inverse relationship between *comfort in exercising influence* and *perceived impact*. And the implications of this decision making scales up beyond reviews of individual books. While critics believe that they are exercising their power as a balance or corrective to the superstar structure of the literary field, their decisions may in fact be reproducing it.

Research shows that the most compelling and consequential reviews come not just from their being positive or negative but from their being those that generate the most discussion:[13] it is an attentional economy, first and foremost. And the punch-up-never-down principle can affect the composition of opinions that we encounter as readers: specifically, while we are more likely to hear strong reactions (positive or negative) about famous people or highly anticipated books by virtue of punching up, the norms against punching down relegate the majority of book reviews written about newer authors to a gray area of descriptive politeness. This exacerbates the inequality of attention given to high-status and low-status writers.

And so, while critics describe attempting to use reviews of superstar works as an opportunity to critique the superstar structure the effect can be that punching up actually reinforces it. The book review world is about grabbing and steering readers' attention: the selling review is the one that gets people talking about particular books, writers, and even reviewers. Thus, writing highly opinionated reviews of books by superstar authors while writing more coy, but ultimately forgettable, reviews of other books may be having the opposite effect intended by reviewers.

Conclusion

Book reviewing contributes to the broader superstar structure of publishing. While reviewers are critical of this system, they do not typically have control over whether a book gets a review. They do, however, control how books by new and more established writers are treated in reviews.

The practice of punching up can be a matter of social-literary conscience: being openly critical of famous authors is framed as a way of striking back at what many reviewers see as the inequities of the status-attainment process in publishing. Critics sometimes veered from this practice depending on the status of the publication they were writing for. In one instance, a reviewer explained that he had no problem writing a very critical review of a newer writer because the review featured in a low-status publication with a small readership. Therefore, the review would not have an impact on the author, or on the overall publishing status ladder, since the reviewer anticipated that no one was going to read it anyways.[14] So there was variation in when and how critics applied the "punch up, never down" double standard.

But the question still remains: why, in most instances, do critics not experience the same kind of anxiety or expect the same kinds of backlash when critiquing powerful people? The findings in this chapter contrast with those in the previous chapter with respect to reviewers' trepidation to be too negative in their reviews. In this context, how can we understand the reason for the persistence of this double standard?

Considering the perceived risks, such as fear of retributive reviewing, writing a negative review of a very famous author may be safer than punching down or even across for a several reasons. First, the odds of the favor being returned are relatively low. It is only on rare occasions that very famous authors write reviews. Several editors mention that they would ideally love to have "celebrity novelists that everyone knows [to review], you know, the Toni Morrisons, John Updikes and those kinds of people." However, the vast majority of reviews are likely to be written by midlist authors. So the favor of a negative review of a famous author is unlikely to be returned, so to speak.

Second, just as critics expressed their adherence to the customary norm of noblesse oblige, wherein people of higher status are expected to act generously toward those "below" them, to describe why they go easy on less established authors, one could reasonably expect that this same principle would be applied to them as midlist writers in relation to superstar novelists. The expectation of noblesse oblige by high-status actors generalizes beyond the case of book reviewing. As Hahl and Zuckerman explain, "the onus is placed on the high-status actor to avoid any action that might threaten the dignity of the low-status actor, else he be suspect of being inconsiderate and inauthentic."[15] Hence, the customary norm against punching down also applies to superstar authors in relation to the less famous writers who are reviewing their works.

Another explanation for why critics are willing to be openly critical of high-status authors is that the perceived benefits for being critical of famous authors may outweigh any potential risks. There are potential advantages to being critical of famous writers. Reviewers also noted that taking down a famous author in a review could be an easy way for struggling writers to "make a splash" or "make a name" for themselves.[16] Just as it is true that very famous authors' books are viewed as events in the literary world and are very likely to be widely read, it is also true that reviews of these same books are likely to be widely read as well. Therefore, critics that go against the grain of literary status and are seen as calling out even elite, famous authors for less than stellar work may gain their own status for doing so, much in the same way that the boy who pointed to the fact that the emperor wore no clothes was lauded for his clear sight and courage.

In other words, the two scenarios are characterized by different degrees of social uncertainty. When punching down or even across, critics imagined a range of potentially undesirable responses on the part of those reviewed, as described in the previous chapter. When punching up, however, the potential rewards are greater, and the odds of retribution are lower, because of same norms that prohibit midlist reviewers from punching down at new writers.

When reviewing superstar writers, critics can be relatively more certain about the risks and rewards that they face if they choose to write a negative review—and are emboldened to do so.

Part 3

Institutional Uncertainty

IN PART 3, we explore the institutional uncertainty facing book reviewing. Institutional uncertainty refers to the relative lack of taken-for-granted procedures, routines, and structures that organize critics' experiences and activities as reviewers.

Consider, for instance, how critics responded to the range of uncertainties and accompanying dilemmas described thus far. On the epistemic front, critics face challenges in determining their "fit" when deciding to accept a review as well as in determining how to justify their judgment. On the social front, critics confront the dilemma of how to handle potential risks to their reputation and professional goals when faced with writing a negative review. There is no formalized institutional guidance dictating how critics should respond to these situations. While informal norms, such as not punching down, informed critics' behavior, these types of constraints are different than, for instance, a governing professional association codifying best practices and sanctioning reviewers who do not adhere to its principles. One can find stand-alone essays, books, and even syllabi about book reviewing; however, theirs are suggestions, and the plurality of contents further underscores that there are no clear guidelines for how to be a critic.

In this final section, then, we attend to how high levels of institutional uncertainty shape the ways critics understand the meaning and value of their work as reviewers: first, at the level of individual critics' explanations for why they review at all; and second, in more existential terms, regarding why critics think we need reviews at all. While the informal organization of reviewing contributes to a lack of coherence and identification with the role of reviewing, reviewers bring their own meanings to the task.

Chapter 6

I Am Not a Critic

MANY RESPONDENTS EXPRESSED some uncertainty about whether they "counted" as reviewers or critics when first invited to be part of this study.[1] Their uncertainty may seem surprising given that, alongside my following the rigors of social scientific sampling procedures, only individuals who had published reviews in the most culturally prominent and elite review outlets in North America, if not the entire English-speaking field of publishing were contacted. If these individuals were unsure if they could be called reviewers, then who could? Critics' immediate uncertainty about whether they counted as such made sense, however, given that the vagueness or ambiguity around who is a critic, which is part of the institutional uncertainty of reviewing.

Critics feel very little *groupness*,[2] that is, they do not have a sense of book reviewing as a bounded category to which they feel belonging. There are no formally defined criteria or processes in place for demarcating who is qualified to do the work of book reviewing. Book critics do have a professional association in the United States. The National Book Critics Circle (NBCC, http://bookcritics.org) offers guidance on reviewing, discussion groups, discounts on literary magazines, and other benefits and services to its members. And we can see from the mandate of this group how the definition of membership casts a very wide net:

> The NBCC serves nearly 600 member *critics*, *authors*, literary *bloggers*, book *publishing personnel*, and student members. Membership in the NBCC is open to *freelance* and *staff* book reviewers at various stages in their careers, associate nonvoting members, and student members. (emphasis added)

The group does not, however, have the power to formally restrict anyone from engaging in book reviewing. There is no regulation that says only registered members of this professional organization can offer book-reviewing services in the same way that medical accreditation prohibits others from offering medical advice. The lack of formal means of demarcating who is or is not a book reviewer leaves this category of work particularly vulnerable to the legitimacy claims of "outsiders" such as amateur reviewers. But it also has implications for how critics position themselves and how critics conceptualize group "insiders."

In this chapter, I explore the source of this lack of groupness. One source of this lack of groupness is the porousness[3] of the boundaries that encircle journalistic reviewing as a particular type of reviewing. Another source regards the informal organization of book reviewing as a form of work; specifically, the increasing reliance on freelance labor. I find that reviewers do not express a strong identification with the role of reviewing or as reviewers.[4,5] But they do bring other meanings and motivations to their task.

What's in a Name? The Porous Boundaries of Journalistic Reviewing

In everyday parlance, some may speak of "critics writing reviews." But many respondents were unclear if either professional moniker rightly applied to them. Their uncertainty relates to the common conflation of the two terms and ambiguity surrounding what differentiates types of criticism. To review briefly, the typology of criticism offered earlier included three different branches of reviewing (discussed in chapter 1): (i) journalistic criticism, whose practitioners have been the focus of this book, (ii) literary essays, and (iii) academic criticism. The degree of specialization in terms of the range of books considered, the intended audience, venues of publication, the qualities of the people who produce them, and their power of consecration is what differentiates each form of reviewing.

Much ink has been spilled over determining the difference between reviewers and reviewing, on the one hand, and critics and criticism, on the other. In addition to the above points, for some, the difference lies in length: reviews are shorter compositions, and criticism is a long form. Others emphasize differences in scope or content:

reviews focus on individual books, while criticism tends to be more reflective and may discuss multiple pieces, a variety of themes, and issues altogether beyond the art pieces under consideration. Yet others emphasize that reviewers are like reporters covering news on a work; any hint of judgment is when reviewing crosses over into criticism.[6]

What specific criteria others have used to differentiate reviewing and criticism is less important for the present discussion than the fact that this fuzziness contributed to respondents' uncertainty about who was a critic, whether they belonged to the institution of literary criticism, and the extent to which they identified with the role of book reviewer even while engaged in writing reviews.

More than a matter of ambiguous nomenclature, reviewers' uncertainty about whether they counted as such also relates to the fact that the boundaries surrounding *journalistic* reviewing as a category are particularly porous among the various types of criticism. While many critics may, in fact, have degrees in English, reviewers did not suggest that an English degree should be a definitive threshold for vetting who would make a qualified critic.[7] There is even some resistance against accreditation.[8] This is unlike the case of academic critics who typically hold a PhD and a university affiliation.

Movement between branches of reviewing also illuminates the porousness of the journalistic reviewer category. Academic critics may choose to enter the world of journalistic reviewing and write reviews for general interest review publications, like a newspaper or a literary magazine, but such movement is one way only: reviewers without the appropriate academic credentials are restricted from engaging in academic criticism.

When it comes to literary essays, there are similarly no formal barriers to engage in this form of reviewing. Yet, the boundaries surrounding journalistic reviewing still prove to be more porous because of the degree of overlap between the book coverage offered by journalistic and reader-reviews: specifically, covering newly published books to help readers find books they might like to read.

Consider, for instance, how one critic articulates the goals of writing (journalistic) book reviews as compared with the writing literary essays. "The principal question that is motivating the piece you're writing is different." He continues: "The question that you have underlying the review is this: The reader is trying to decide whether to buy this book." In contrast, "literary [essayistic] criticism is, as I read it, something that is itself a form of literature in which the subject is, more than anything else, an opportunity for the critic to display his or her genius." Specifically, he offered the following example:

> When I read—just to give an example—Michael Hoffman's review of Martin Amis' most recent book, which was quite scathing, I didn't come away with it thinking, "Boy, this Martin Amis book is crap." I came away from it thinking, "Boy, Michael Hoffman is a great critic."

The critic distinguishes between journalistic and essayistic criticism in terms of the imagined "takeaway" of the reader.

Another critic offered a similar distinction focusing on the fact that different publications have different audiences, which warrant different approaches to writing about books:

> I'm aware that the reader of the *New York Times* is someone whose basic decision is, "Am I going to buy this book?" . . . Now if I was writing for, say, *The Nation* . . . you approach it from a very different standpoint because first of all the book is probably being reviewed at least six months after its publication. The readership is smaller and more intellectual . . . people who like to read essays, who like to read about literature. They're not necessarily people who are simply trying to decide which novel to read next.

The readers of literary essays are, here, imagined to be people who have a more specialized interest in reading in-depth essays about books. In contrast, no such assumption is made of the readers of journalistic book reviewers, who are instead presumed to be receptive to reading recommendations. It is this overlap in the market intermediary function of journalistic and amateur reviews that leaves journalistic reviewing uniquely vulnerable to contest and encroachment from amateur reviewers in ways that literary essayists and academic forms of criticism are not.

In the absence of formal legal regulations demarcating who can or cannot practice as a book reviewer, respondents do draw cultural boundaries between what they do and what average readers have to offer in their reviews. Critics often used the terms "bloggers" or "online" reviews as colloquial euphemisms for amateurs, though whether reviews appeared in print or digital formats was not a defining boundary. Indeed, many critics write reviews for publications that appear across both media. Instead, the main boundary is the one that separates people who review as a hobby or for recreation on one side, and those who review as part of a broader professional life with books and writing, on the other.

Keen defines an amateur as "a hobbyist, someone who does not make a living from his or her field of interest, a lay person, lacking credentials, a dabbler."[9,10] Critics frequently imagined and described amateur reviewers as inhabiting nonprofessional spaces as a way of underlining their recreational involvement in book culture. For example, when describing amateur reviewers, critics often imagined them as writing from their parents' basement (they also imagined them to be living there), on their laptops at coffee shops, or at home, as implied by the image of the amateur as "a guy in his pajamas."

Some critics go even further in invoking domestic imagery to draw the boundary between professional and amateur reviewers. One critic described the people posting reviews on Goodreads.com as "just a bunch of moms." Another reviewer who lamented the state of book reviewing online clarified that while she "love[s] Salon, and Laura Miller,"[11] she takes issue with "these mom and pop sort of blogs that people have, they've thrown it together, a *WordPress* kind of thing" where they "might also be writing recipes for lemonade."

Far from hobbyists, fiction critics view themselves (and are viewed by others) as connoisseurs: individuals with specialized knowledge of literature, which enables them to appraise and appreciate books in ways that the average reader cannot.[12,13] And while critics could not evoke formal credentials to distinguish what they did from amateur reviewers, they did draw on abstract notions of commitment and dedication to the world of books to suggest why their ranks should be closed off from the average reader. For example, one critic expressed the belief that such cultural competency was gained through their prolonged and formal engagement with books as people who "make a career of thinking about [books]" through their work, whether as novelists, teachers, academics, or journalists rather than on a recreational basis. Another critic compared the situation of writing reviews to writing music where anyone can just go "into their garage and recor[d] a song." He states that he would rather listen to a song by "someone who's been working at this for ten years" or someone who has "spent the 10,000 hours[14] [to] get really good at something."

Implicit here is a boundary between people who participate in book culture as a hobby (such as amateurs) and people who somehow make a career related to writing or books more generally (such as novelists, academics, journalists, etc.). We see this distinction in the comments of one reviewer who characterized the difference between hobbyists and people who get "paid a living wage" to write about books this way:

> [Y]ou might know a great deal about, you know, cell biology, but you don't know as much as an actual cell biologist because that's what they do all day. So if it's just your hobby, if you're a book blogger as your hobby, it's just not the same job as it is to know about all the books that are coming out and who are the writers that people are talking about.

Yet, it is notable that most "professional" reviewers also do not review regularly, and even fewer are "paid a living wage." Many were not full-time reviewers or reviewed with less frequency—perhaps writing only a few reviews in the past year. Indeed, only ten respondents could be characterized as having held, at some point in time, a full-time position related to book reviewing. The editor for a major East Coast newspaper book section estimated there are probably only twelve full-time critics left in America; other informants estimated it could not be "more than a handful." Taken less literally, then, critics use the seriousness of their *intention* as another way to draw symbolic boundaries between themselves and amateurs.

Yet, critics' comments about the occupational organization of reviewing as a form of work alludes to the second source of uncertainty contributing to critics' lack of a sense of groupness: book reviewing is rarely a full-time job.

Reviewing on the Side: The Conversion Value of Reviewing

The structure of book reviewing as a form of work follows the growing trend of contingent labor, wherein individuals are brought in and let go as employers' needs wax and wane. The world of newspaper publishing, which is the traditional organizational basis of book reviewing, has undergone radical transformation.[15] Newspapers have greatly diminished the space allotted for book reviewing, with many stand-alone book sections being folded into general entertainment sections because of the changing economics of print publishing. With less space for book reviews, among other factors, there are fewer review assignments and a lower demand for full-time book critics on staff.

One strategy publications have used to adapt to this precarious economic climate is increasing reliance on nonstaff freelance reviewers who offer more flexibility than in-house critics. Most critics are thus employed on a single-assignment basis. For many critics then, it is not clear when the next review assignment will appear, or even which publication they will take their reviewing talents to. Nor are critics beholden to particular review outlets. This trend is true even with expansions in web-based reviewing over recent years. Print publications are expanding their news editions online: the *New Yorker*, for instance, now publishes many reviews online alongside its printed edition. Additionally, new web-based outlets such as *n+1* and Slate .com or the *New Inquiry* have created new opportunities for book reviewing online. However, even in these new venues, there is a reliance on book reviewers on a freelance basis. This is true for journalists that work for online newsrooms in general.[16]

Reviewing is not a primary work activity; it is something reviewers do "on the side" of their other professional activities from which they earn their living. This status contributes to the lack of identification with, and sense of, book reviewing as a distinct occupational group expressed by so many respondents. Few identified first or foremost as book reviewers when I asked critics to describe their professional activities which is another reason that respondents were uncertain about whether or not they qualified as critics for the purpose of this study. Instead, they identified first with their work as academics, creative writing teachers, journalists, or writers and then wrote reviews on an occasional basis.

The following list contains respondents' descriptions of how they earned a living, as well as their primary activities, in their own words:

"I'm primarily a book writer."

"I'm a book author. . . . Every so often I'm asked to do a book review but . . . I wouldn't say that's my main job, I'd say my main job is being a book writer."

"I am a freelance journalist, and also a book reviewer."

"I'm a columnist and critic."

"I review books for a number of places. . . . I also write essays. . . . I was an English professor [and] have a book coming out."

"I'm mostly a writer . . . and I occasionally write book reviews, as well as essays and occasional journalism, but mostly—I spend most of my days working on fiction."

"Well, I'm primarily a novelist and a writer. . . . I also teach creative writing . . . and I occasionally review books."

"I teach. . . . I mostly write. . . . I also do reviews."

Some respondents neglected to identify themselves as critics altogether. One reviewer explained: "Well, I guess there are two facets to my life. One, I'm a college professor and I teach English. . . . The other main professional activity, I'm a writer of fiction." This pattern is particularly revealing given that my respondents were primed by the fact that I was interviewing them for a study on book reviewing.

It is common for people in creative fields to be engaged in multiple forms of work, which they combine to earn a living.[17,18] These supplementary forms of work are sometimes referred to as secondary artistic or para-artistic jobs.[19] Menger anticipates that approximately 10 percent of artists live "exclusively from their art."[20] In this context, reviewing can be understood as a secondary artistic activity for people engaged in literary creation or journalism and who face a lack of certainty relating to economic outcomes and success. One possible explanation is that it is a rational response to dealing with the economic insecurity of being a writer—or so the "occupational diversification" argument would go.

But this does not adequately convey the situation of many reviewers. When I asked reviewers why they chose to take on the extra task of reviewing on the side of their regular activities, the answer was rarely pecuniary. Most of the people I interviewed who wrote reviews did not fit the stereotype of the starving artist but earned their living through other professional activities, such as teaching in universities. Finding alternative sources of income was not identified as a primary motivation for engaging in book reviewing in part because reviewing does not pay well. As one reviewer who is also a novelist noted: "[Reviewing is] not a well-paying job, considering how much time you have to spend reading the book, processing the book and then writing about the book. Financially you are better off working in the 7-Eleven." Instead, critics find nonmonetary forms of profit from engaging in book reviewing. Below I identify some of these other benefits. And while specifics vary, the overall pattern is that critics often framed their reviewing work as operating in service of their identities and practices as writers.

For the Love of Reading: Reviewing
as a Pathway to Self-Cultivation

The most readily given response for what kept reviewers engaged in the reportedly time-consuming and low-paying activity of book reviewing was a love of reading or a "love of the novel." One reviewer simply explained: "I like reading books," and "I like thinking about books." Of course, book reviewing is not the only way to participate in reading and thinking about books.

Critics described the experience of reading a book with an eye toward writing a review as different to that of reading as a private consumer. Specifically, the difference concerned the fact that they are required to read in a more contemplative way, which ultimately enriched their reading experience. One critic explained:

> I like reviewing because I really do find myself much more in-volved in a book when I write about it. Just thinking about a book for a couple of weeks, and how to clear up my thoughts on the page, makes my experience with the book much deeper and much more rewarding.

Similarly, another reviewer described her engagement with review-ing as "kind of selfish" because "it helps me think about what I've read [and] deepens my personal reading experience by reviewing books."

But what does this deepened reading experience entail? Ultimately, reviewers try to provide context and analysis of the books that they read. This process is creatively and intellectually demanding and requires deeper thought about a book than when reading for personal enjoyment. Take, for example, the variety of strategies reviewers used, including reading the book multiple times and reading previous books written by the author whose current work is under review—in the case of second and third-plus books—in order to prepare for the review-writing process and to provide a context and analysis of the books they review.

The editorial structure of reviewing discussed in chapter 2—the fact that books are assigned to reviewers by editors—gives critics an opportunity to extend themselves beyond their usual reading habits. This was an attractive feature for reviewers who consider themselves avid and curious readers. Many reviewers expressed delight at being exposed to new genres and new ideas through the review assignment process. As one critic noted: reviewing "allows me to read books that I might not necessarily get to" not only because of time constraints but also because editors sometimes chose books they might not have themselves selected.

Another reviewer I spoke with runs her own book review section, which means she could assign herself any book she would like to review. Yet, she enjoys doing reviewing assignments for other editors precisely because of the unpredictability of the review assignment she will receive. She explained: "I review books for [other review sections] and, again, part of the thing I enjoy about that actually is having somebody else make the choice for me. I'[m] often given things that I would never choose to give myself."

Another reviewer went as far as to liken the experience of receiving review assignments to Christmas morning:

> It's always still a little Christmas-like, and even if the book sort of seems like, "Well, maybe, this is a genre that I don't really love a whole lot," I always feel that every book is going to teach me something. . . . *It never feels like work that is without value.* (emphasis added)

The specific value that reviewers identified was the fact that reviewing stretched them intellectually, with the above critic stretching himself beyond his regular reading habits by venturing into "a genre that [he didn't] really love a whole lot." Similarly, another critic, who also holds a full-time academic post, explained: "It challenges me to look at materials I probably would not have looked at otherwise. It *extends* me" (emphasis added). Alongside reading broadly and "making discoveries of authors, or subjects that are new" as reasons for reviewing, another reviewer explained that he enjoys reviewing because it gives him "the chance to think deeply and critically about a work of art." This idea that reading for the purpose of reviewing "extends," cultivates, or teaches reviewers is tied to the particular valuation of books as a form of extracurricular or recreational activity. Literacy is overwhelmingly viewed as a social good. And among the different forms of literacy, *literary reading* is perhaps the most sacred and revered form.[21]

Highbrow art is conventionally seen as fare that is rich and complex; the challenging nature of the art is part of the beauty of work in the realm (such as in interpretive dance). Highbrow art is intended to elicit an engaging intellectual experience.[22,23] In contrast, lowbrow fare is considered facile, and the main goal is unmediated enjoyment—there is no need for critics to do any extra interpretive work. As the main goal is entertainment and easy enjoyment, the only relevant criterion is whether the partaker liked it or not (more on this in the next chapter).

Being "a reader" confers a degree of social honor on individuals since literary reading has historically been associated with intellectualism and a form of *cultural cultivation*.[24,25] This cultivating quality of reading as a form of social practice is only intensified by the review experience as reviewing *deepens* the reading experience: it is effortful and is an intellectual and interpretive exercise.

Critics thus describe reviewing as presenting a learning opportunity: the act of preparing for and writing a review tasks reviewers with increasing their breadth as readers and invites them to examine works beyond their normal reading habits. And critics frame these opportunities as valuable. These descriptions also resonate with the idea of reviewing as an opportunity to accrue cultural capital in that through reviewing reviewers are able to broaden their literary horizons by extending themselves beyond their cultural comfort zones. In this way, reviewing served critics' self-concepts as intellectually curious and culturally enriched people.

For the Love of Writing: Reviewing
as a Pathway to an Improved Craft

Another reason critics gave for taking on the labor of reviewing was that it provided them with the opportunity to cultivate themselves, not just as book readers, but as writers as well. In other words, part of what critics say they most enjoy about reviewing and why they engage in it is that it allowed them to hone their independent writing practice. For example, one reviewer, who had written multiple books, explained that reviewing was "part of my learning as a writer." He further explained that putting together a review required him to study the books very carefully: "when I'm writing a review, I study how they're put together, so I do learn a little bit from the reviews that I write, not just about the book themselves but also how those books are written." This reviewer's comments echo back to the idea that reviewing requires a kind of reading that is deeper than how one might otherwise read a book when reading just for pleasure.

Another critic explained that what she finds most enjoyable and beneficial about reviewing is that it helps her learn: "when you're writing novels and not just reviewing, part of what you do when you look at something that really works, and try to figure out how it works, it's a constant learning process for the writer." Specifically, she often looked at different elements of the "toolkit of [the] craft," including the pacing of a story and the use of flashback. Bringing their knowledge and writerly outlook to the reading and deconstruction of books is not only for the sake of writing a review; it is also to accumulate cultural resources or knowledge, in the form of a deeper appreciation of the craft of fiction and an intuitive understanding of what makes fiction work, which they can use to inform their role as writers.

A slightly different example of this writerly impetus to self-improvement comes from a critic who makes his living as a professor. He confessed that what he finds the most enjoyable and what he finds the most challenging about reviewing is the same: "The deadlines, the quick writing, the pressure to get it out a little more quickly than you would like to." He explained:

> I think that we in the academy tend to work at a much more measured pace. Sometimes that's a good thing. Sometimes that's not a good thing, but to get a good review out and make it good, and get it done on time, and to meet a deadline, really requires that you stay on your toes, and I think that's a good thing. It's a good habit, particularly for academics like me to cultivate.

Here we see the familiar emphasis on how skills developed through his experiences with reviewing—in this case a kind of time management and expediency with making complicated arguments—that is not usually required according to the pacing of academic publishing. The academic here is not trying to become more familiar with writing fiction as an artistic craft, still, the emphasis is on developing a skill or competency through reviewing that he is able to bring back and apply to his scholarly writing. It is a writing skill that can be developed through reviewing to create some positive value and incentive for undertaking the labor of writing reviews in absence of financial incentives.

Critics also benefitted not only from a closer examination of the themes and content of books under review, but also from examining what makes a book work. For example, one reviewer explained that reviewing offers him "a chance, not only to read a book and write a review, *but to learn*, to look at that book and try and figure out what makes it work, or why did I think it didn't work" (emphasis added). More than as broadening or deepening the reading experience, many critics frame the value of their labor as reviewers as helping them to improve their craft as writers. It is through effortful self-study of the crafting of books and analysis of what makes them work that reviewers are able to improve their own acumen as writers.

For the Love of One's Name in Print: Reviewing as Belonging

Critics also had more nakedly extrinsic and less educative motivations for reviewing, including increased visibility and publicity within the literary community. For some, reviewing was a required part of membership in the wider literary community and what was entailed in being a member in good standing within that group.

Given the switch-role reward structure (chapter 4) of reviewing, writing reviews is an act of professional obligation and courtesy exercised by members of the literary community. A fellow reviewer similarly expressed that just as he hoped that his own books would be reviewed when they were published, "it didn't make any sense to me to [not] return the favor by discussing the work of my contemporaries." So, for many, reviewing was part of what it meant to be an active writer in the literary community.

But what it means to be a writer is unclear, as the boundaries of that category can be quite blurry as well. For many, seeing one's name signed on a review served as an objectified signal of one's belonging to the wider literary community. One reviewer, who is also a novelist and a professor of creative writing, explained how reviewing fit into her broader professional profile. She began with the familiar characterization of book reviewing as being time-consuming with little economic pay off ("Certainly there's no financial incentive to do it. You get paid virtually nothing"). She then went on to explain that she reviews because she "wanted to be part of the literary community, and be part of the discussion about books, about literature, about what was happening in literature today." Reviewing helps her to feel like she is part of the literary conversation.

Reviewing also facilitated respondents' feeling of membership in the literary community because reviewing helped critics to bring attention to and feature their work as writers, or what they do when they are not writing reviews. Many other critics voiced that reviewing was an effective way of keeping their names "in the public eye" given that it can often be many years before their books come out. This was enticing enough to convince some writers who actually don't enjoy writing reviews to continue doing so, anyway.

Another critic expressed a similar hope for his work as a reviewer. Specifically, in addition to informing the public what a book is about and whether it is worth reading, "you're hoping that people are not only going to notice that book review because of what you wrote about, but because you wrote it and people would hopefully be interested in other pieces that you have written." Critics were therefore aware that book reviews could bring publicity not only for the new book being reviewed, but also for the person writing the review and that person's own work as a writer and thinker. Reviewing thus has a double-publicity potential: not only to publicize the book that is formally under review but also to publicize the work of the reviewer— who is often also a working writer.

Beyond using the review as a simple reminder to others of one's existence, reviews represented an opportunity to demonstrate reviewers' writerly and intellectual talents and to actively attract new readers to the critic's work elsewhere, such as their own published books. The following critic, a well-known novelist with more than six books to her name, speaks to this publicizing effect with reference to reviewers' bylines that appear at the bottom of their articles:

> If you're a person who reads book reviews then you think, "Well, oh look, here's a review by [X], so *The New York Times* asked her to write this. She really must be a good writer. . . . I should go read—you know, I forgot that I really like her writing, and what's the name of that book? Oh, here it is, right here [the byline]."

The publicity that comes with reviewing is not always self-serving, however. One reviewer, who is also the author of four books and reviews only a handful books in any given year, confessed: "to be totally honest, [reviewing is] the hardest thing I do, and I don't really enjoy it that much. I do it because . . . it's a way for me to interact with the literary community in a more public way." Not only was writing books a time-consuming affair; it was also a lonely one. This critic's desire to interact with the literary community stemmed from the reality of her daily life as a writer: "It's very solitary to be writing in your office five hours every day and this is one way to be, at least in some way to sort of have your name circulating and to have a more public forum." And reviewing offered a brief reprieve from the solitude and long stretches of invisibility that come with the work of writing. These are other ways that reviewing complemented the workflow of people's writing lives, and how many critics saw reviewing as fitting into their work as writers, first and foremost.

We saw in chapter 4 that producing a good article is part of what reviewers attempt to do when writing reviews (the analytical and entertainment objectives). However, these imperatives can be taken too far if critics' comments—and in particular, their writing style— take attention away from the book and draw too much attention to the reviewers themselves, though exactly how to balance the two types of publicizing functions is experienced by many reviewers as a personal decision. In keeping with the high degree of institutional uncertainty characterizing book reviewing, there are no formal guidelines or procedures for determining whether the dual projects of highlighting a book and featuring one's own acumen are achieved in an acceptable manner. But if the right balance is struck, then reviewing can be a profitable endeavor, though not in the traditionally economic sense of the term.

———————

Part of the reason that financial capital was not a strong incentive for reviewing was because it was largely an activity that people engaged in alongside a broader portfolio of professional activities. One reviewer made this explicit: "I think, for me, the money from reviews is not as important either because I have sources of [income]." Specifically, this reviewer earned her living through other book-related activities. While accruing financial capital was clearly not a primary motivation for why critics engaged in reviewing, what becomes apparent is that critics are compensated with other types of rewards or capital.

Following Bourdieu, the term "capital" refers to the different types of valued social resources.[26] Capital takes multiple forms in addition to financial resources. Briefly, *human* capital refers to the knowledge, skills, or habits that result in some kind of advantage or value.[27] A common form of human capital comes in the form of educational credentials. *Cultural* capital refers to advantageous knowledge and competencies we often associate with "cultivated" or otherwise "cultured" people and activities, such as knowledge about books or wine. *Social* capital comprises the social connections individuals share with others and the potential resources that are facilitated by membership in networks, such as learning about reviewing opportunities. And *symbolic* capital refers broadly to a "capital of trust" or recognition of legitimacy, which often depends on a distancing from economic motives.[28]

Part of the analytical utility of thinking about different forms of capital is to consider the extent to which they are interconvertible;[29] that is, how one form of capital can be converted into another. As we see above, for some critics, there is the hope that reviewing a book will raise awareness of their work elsewhere. One critic recalled pitching a review for a newspaper and reflected that "writing a piece for them put me on their radar," after which her book was reviewed in the same publication. For yet other critics, reviewing could beget future reviewing opportunities at other publications as reviewers became known commodities. In this way, the visibility of reviewing could translate into future work opportunities. Critics also hoped that the quality of reviews would also the draw attention of future readers, which could have the potential of converting into future book sales.

There are also symbolic profits to be had, encapsulated by the idea of being part of the literary community. While critics emphasized the time and effort they put into reviewing and the aesthetic pleasures and skills they reaped from these labors, these cultural competencies also make them privileged people authorized to do this kind of work; in other words, they are legitimizing not only the book but also themselves[28] as speaking on behalf of good fiction.

Conclusion

Beyond exploring the nonmonetary profits of reviewing or the conversion value of reviewing, another contribution of this chapter is that we see how respondents' professional identities are not rooted in being a book reviewer. Instead, they are rooted in their work as academics, creative writing teachers, journalists—and especially, writers. Indeed, when I asked why critics declined to review books, the answers often concerned scenarios where accepting the assignment would have unjustifiably interfered with their other projects; the most common reason for declining a review was that the money was not worth the time that the review would take away from writing or related professional activities.

Critics' lack of identification with the reviewer role may be intuitively understood as a function of the fact that reviewing is not the primary way they earn their living. However, research elsewhere has established how individuals maintain a strong sense of identification with roles even when they are nonpaying or otherwise nonprimary work activities.[30] I have suggested instead that critics' lack of identification with reviewing is tied to the lack of groupness. And this is symptomatic of the high degree of institutional uncertainty that characterizes reviewing as a form of work; specifically, the porousness of its boundaries and—but not exclusively—its freelance structure.

We have seen throughout the empirical chapters how critics are primed to think of themselves as writers, in particular, at virtually every stage of their review process: this begins at the outset when critics explained why they think they are invited to review (often based on similarities between their own writing and the work under consideration, as we saw in chapter 2); the unique competencies they bring to the task (a writerly eye and sensibility, as discussed in chapters 2 and 3); and the weighed professional and emotional impact of their reviews as a result of the switch-role reward structure (explored in chapters 4 and 5).

In the absence of formalized routines, procedures, and other sources of institutional guidance, critics draw on alternative and readily accessible identities to bring coherence to their experience as reviewers. Taken together, the previous and current chapters demonstrate how critics' roles as writers become a conceptual anchor that frames the consequences and meanings of their actions in their capacity as reviewers. And as we will see in the final chapter, critics' multiple entanglements with the book reviewing field—as writers and as reviewers—also come to bear on their answers to the question of why we need book reviews at all.

Chapter 7

Do We Need Book Reviews?

IN THIS PENULTIMATE CHAPTER, we zoom out to deal with institutional uncertainty in more existential terms and consider critics' answers to the questions: What is the value of book reviewing, and why have reviewing at all? A general feeling of pessimism and alarm about the state of book reviewing pervades public discourse. This sentiment is captured by communications scholar Maarit Jaakkola[1] with a survey of newspaper and magazine articles reflecting on arts criticism from the past decade:

> [They are] endowed with emblematic titles such as "The Crisis of Criticism,"[2] "What Happened to Art Criticism?,"[3] "Critical Mess,"[4] "The Death of the Critic,"[5] "Faint Praise: The Plight of Book Reviewing in America,"[6] and "The State of Art Criticism."[7]

And even more academic-oriented works take up the topic, purporting to deal with the crisis of reviewing's legitimacy—the present analysis included.

Much of the current book crisis discourse has focused on the impact of large-scale economic and technological shifts enabled by digitization. On the economic front, essays in the media have posited that book review sections do not attract enough advertising dollars to remain financially viable. Some argue[8,9,10] that this loss of advertising dollars by newspapers is itself tied to dwindling book sales in the broader publishing world related to reduced readership, which hollows out the marketing budgets of publishing companies that might otherwise purchase advertisements in reviewing pages. The result is that there are fewer opportunities for reviewing. Technological developments, including the rise of new micromedia for raising awareness about books, also features prominently in the crisis narrative of book reviewing: the internet has created opportunities for everyday readers to engage in public and mass dissemination of their responses to books, and this has spurred a related cultural crisis in which the legitimacy and utility of professional book reviewers are in question.

Yet, contrary to popular understandings, economic and technological transformations were not the most salient concerns among the critics I interviewed when asked about their view of the current state of book reviewing. Distinctions between online and offline, new media and legacy media, or digital and print are not the relevant battle lines when discussing the value and future legitimacy of book reviewing. Critics were more likely to locate the threats to the unique value and mission of journalistic criticism in the practices of other types of reviewers—and not just amateurs.

The Value of Book Reviewing

Although respondents do not identify closely or feel a sense of groupness as book reviewers, this does not mean that they had clarity about the value and contribution of reviewing itself. Indeed, book reviewing is experiencing unsettled times, when understandings previously taken for granted (including the significance of reviews) are in flux and up for debate. Critics thus have need to become more clear-eyed and more explicit about the legitimacy and contribution of their work when such meanings appear up for negotiation.

I argue that the particular value of journalistic book reviewing in the eyes of reviewers was as a genre of literary evaluation that treats literary fiction as, at once, a rarified art form and as an essential part of the social fabric of our everyday life. Critics typically articulated this distinct value of their work by contrasting it with the perceived failings and threats posed by two other types of reviewing: amateur and academic review practices.

Amateurs and The Threat of Lowbrowing Reviews

The idea that arts journalism is in crisis is not new, but more of a perennial concern.[11] Yet talk of crisis in the history of journalism often becomes especially visible whenever there are introductions of new technology.[12] For example, the abilities of radio[13] and television[14] to "break" news in a timely manner were once conceptualized as competitive threats to the viability of traditional newspapers. More recently, the rise of online spaces for average readers to disseminate their own opinions about books, whether through social network sites like Goodreads or online marketplaces, have come to the fore. While the specifics may vary, during times of change, feelings of fear and trepidation often coexist with feelings of optimism about what such ruptures between old ways and new ways may bring. It will come as no surprise, then, to learn that newspaper book reviewers view reader-reviewers' entry into the reviewing field with great ambivalence.

Regarding the potential benefits of the increased participation of average readers in the critical discussion of books, one of the most commonly cited virtues of the shifting review landscape is its democratic ethos. The Internet and related media gave voice to the average reader. As one reviewer, reflecting on the rise of amateurs, noted: "I think it's wonderful if people read and come up with their own opinions. I think it's a marvelous thing. There's nothing that says any particular group of people have a monopoly." Yet, this same reviewer quickly undermines this potential with her skepticism about bloggers' actual mental acuity: "I do sometimes think that bloggers are kind of dumb, as a general rule."

Critics could be expected to welcome the participation of average readers giving their opinions about books as especially appreciable by many during a time when reading culture appears to be dwindling in competition with other types of leisure activities. But critics' ambivalent attitudes toward amateur reviewing is informed by a zero-sum framing of the relationship between democratizing the range of voices represented in book discourse and the quality of those expressed thoughts. For example, one reviewer explained: "We maybe have a democratization of what gets written about, which is a good thing. But I think we all, we pay the price in the quality of the writing and the thinking, [which] has diluted as a result." Similarly, another reviewer described the growth of reader reviews and amateur book blogs as "healthy. . . . It is very democratic." He continued, "I'm not in any way against people manifesting, obviously, their opinion about things. This is all for the good." Yet, he is also quick to clarify: "[Amateur reviewing] is more spontaneous reactions to books. I think that a serious book review requires time and energy, dedication."

The characterization of reader reviews as knee-jerk reactions, or as opinions, compared to the "serious" and reasoned discussion of professional reviews, echoes the mass culture critique that reasons that participation in high culture requires serious involvement and intent, whereas participation in mass or popular culture is a passive and superficial affair, if not detrimental to culture and society more generally.[15] An important distinction between the two, however, is that critics' qualms were not about the types of books (i.e., popular genres) individuals were reading, but about *how* readers were engaging with literary fiction as a high-culture genre.

Specifically, critics were concerned that amateur critics were treating books as pieces of *entertainment* rather than as objects of *aesthetic contemplation*.[16] The distinction between entertainment value and aesthetic value, as they are discussed here, informs how consumers engage with the cultural objects. For instance, as discussed in chapter 6, highbrow cultural forms are conventionally appreciated for their richness, complexity, and ability to provide an intellectually and aesthetically challenging experience.[17,18] In contrast, lowbrow cultural fare is considered facile, and concerned primarily with providing consumers with unmediated entertainment and enjoyment. What critics were concerned about, then, was the applying of lowbrow expectations and evaluative criteria to the forms of highbrow literary fiction journalistic reviewers typically cover.

Critics often used Amazon.com as an example of the worst of amateur reviewing and its application of lowbrow evaluative criteria to novels. One critic bemoaned the ways that people on Amazon.com evaluate books:

> The Amazon.com reviewers, it's like they're reviewing a product. It's like they bought a pair of Nikes and they are going on and saying, "Oh, my Nikes feel just great, they fit perfectly and I love them." Then they go on and review a book and say, "Oh, this book was too long, I got really sleepy halfway through," and just stuff like that.

Literally, the reviewer is offended that amateur reviewers treat Nikes and novels as equivalent consumer products. Books, in the minds of reviewers, are qualitatively different from shoes and should be treated as such. For critics, books are forms of art and should be discussed and evaluated in these terms.

In the context of highbrow versus lowbrow evaluative criteria, to say that a book is too long or that it induces sleep, suggests that it may take more than one sitting to complete, and that it may not be an easy read. If the problem with the book is that it makes the reader "sleepy," then the assumption is that the book should provide entertainment or stimulation, and that the reader is a passive consumer waiting to be stimulated by the object.[19]

A related concern is whether reviews like those on Amazon.com can properly meet the needs of the general reading public. One reviewer declared, "If you look at [amateur reviews], you're like, 'That really doesn't tell me what I need to know. It just told me that you liked it or didn't like it.'" The same reviewer continued: "All that 'thumbs up' and 'thumbs down' and all the stars and all that stuff, it's fine, but it's not reviewing." The system of rating via stars and thumbs up or down may be argued by some to minimally fulfill the evaluative function of reviewing, but in ways that fall short of what reviews should offer. Recall in chapters 3 and 4 we saw that critics understand books to be multidimensional (and not reducible to a metric of stars) and that book reviews were seen not only to serve an evaluative function, but also to offer description, analysis, and entertainment; and to be a form of literature in and of itself.

Of not "or" course, not all amateur reviewers were the same. And some critics even ventured to say that amateur reviews they had read (often of their own books) could be very incisive; however, in general, the sheer volume of amateur reviews meant that as a group such reviews were believed to be of lower quality. As one reviewer described it: "the signal-to-noise ratio could be altered more in favor of signal and less towards noise."

Critics' concerns about the quality of amateur reviews went beyond their evaluative bases and extended to the quality of their prose. This occurred by contrasting the imagined practices of amateur reviewers to the normal standards and practices of legacy media, such as print—including the presumed absence of working with an editor. The editor of a newspaper section characterized amateur reviews as "missing the discipline of print," which "at the lowest level [means] that [they] are just too rambling," and without the help of higher levels of editing that they are not too self-absorbed but "turned outward" toward the reader.

Perhaps critics are being unfair in their characterization and exaggerating their fears as a means to protect their cultural turf. But there is data to support what critics are saying about amateur-generated reviews. Research in film has shown that that amateur reviews contained more informal "popular" versus "high-art" evaluative schemas than traditional professional reviews. This difference is said to be driven by a lack of editorial control in amateur reviewing.[20] Another explanation is that amateur reviewers have different goals when writing for nontraditional review spaces such as private blogs. Rather than being a venue where readers can share their critical thoughts, such spaces can simply be a place for book lovers to share and connect with fellow readers.[21]

In essence, critics are concerned with the threat that amateur reviews carry, which is the potential lowbrowing of reviewing in two distinct ways: first, through the employment of inappropriate lowbrow criteria—judging novels for their entertainment value rather than as works of aesthetic contemplation, thereby reducing literary fiction to popular entertainment; and second, through the objects produced—the reviews—which they do not perceive as creating any useful or enjoyable reading experience; therefore, impoverishing literary discourse overall.

A Threat of Irrelevance: Reviewing from the Ivory Tower

If the critics I interviewed were concerned that amateurs did not bring enough analysis to their reading or did not have enough background knowledge or professional training to speak to the artistic significance of books, they also had equal concern about the overintellectualization of book reviewing. Specifically, critics were wary of this tendency in literary academics who did not adequately switch gears when writing for not for academics but book reviews for a general audience. These reviewers were viewed as stuck in "the intellectual weeds."

Academic reviewers influence what goes on in journalistic reviewing by virtue of the fact that it is not uncommon for academic critics to contribute reviews for more general publications, such as newspapers. Many critics are themselves academics whom editors recruit for their literary knowledge, which can be fruitfully applied to book reviewing. Additionally, many academics are themselves published authors, which makes it easier for editors to match them to relevant titles. What is at issue is how and the degree to which literary academics adapt their knowledge and writing to fit the task of *journalistic* reviewing as a distinct branch of criticism and genre.

In conversation, it was common for reviewers to oppose evaluations driven by (overly) intellectualized concerns rather than artistically oriented concerns. The risk of a lack of attention to the artistic qualities of novels posed by academic-styled approaches to reviewing is articulated by a former English professor with the following anecdote he attributed to the reviewer James Wood: If you were to ask a group of graduate students to talk about Jane Austen, then they could speak at length about "gender this, and politics that, and blah, blah." But if you asked them how Austen differentiates the characters in her books, then "they will completely draw a blank." This provocative anecdote illustrates how critics juxtapose academic approaches to reviewing, here equated with politicized and ideological analyses, to concerns of the artistic craft.

And more to the point, such political and ideological analyses are viewed as disconnected from the imagined needs of the average reader. The same reviewer continued, "I don't like to think of books as a specialist, and I don't like to write about them as a specialist. . . . You're [writing for] people who aren't reading because they're specialists, but who are reading because they're general readers who are trying to get some book selected." The problem here, to the journalistic reviewer, is that academic concerns are not concerns of interest to the general reader. This reviewer anchors the distinction between academic-style criticism and what he does in terms of fulfilling the mediating function of reviewing, which is to help steer readers toward books they might like to read.

It was deemed important that academics "code switch" between their regular mode of literary inquiry and a different mode of literary inquiry to meet the needs of a general interest audience. The inability or reluctance to code switch was a source of irritation to some reviewers—not that critics felt that academics should stay out of journalistic reviewing. One reviewer who is himself an academic criticized another academic who also reviews for being too "pretentious in his intellectual outlook" and for being "so above his own readers that in the end, rather than doing a service he does a disservice to the book that he is reviewing." This critic was of the opinion that reviews are not academic essays, and that academics who review on the side need to remember to adjust their tone and concerns when reviewing for general interest audiences—what one reviewer described as reviewing from a "humble" place.

Literary theories were often used as an emblem for academics' overly pedantic and esoteric approach to books. And many respondents had very strong opinions about the inappropriateness of using literary theories as part of their review practice. "Outside of invading small countries, the worst thing that men do is to invent literary theories," explained one respondent who has a PhD in English and had to "sit through all of that stuff." When asked about critics whose work he disliked, another reviewer offered: "I can think of many that are academics that I find absolutely boring because they are trying to fit a book into some sort of theory. And I find that abusive, violent to the book and to the author." Significantly, this critic also teaches literature at a university in Massachusetts, showing that such sentiments were not restricted to people who did not have experiences in academe or in an academic post. Altogether, these reviewers felt that the type of esoteric concerns appropriate for academic criticism should not be transported into journalistic criticism; and this relates to the unique value that journalistic reviewing offers its audience.

The academic critic's perspective was used as a foil for more artistic and emotionally engaged forms of reading offered by the journalistic reviewer. The idea that intellectualized or academic appreciation and artistic appreciation of a book are different was a common characterization. "I think there are two categories of people who are reviewing books. One, is the sort of academic, more professional reviewer," explained one critic. The second category consists of "book reviewers like me who have absolutely no critical history or agenda [and] just react, artistically and emotionally, to the material." Here there is an implied contrast between reviewers like her (a novelist) who take an artistic approach to reviewing, and academic-type reviewers, who take a different approach.

More than a matter of differences in approach, however, reviews rooted in pedantry were seen as doing a service to the general readers of book reviews. Consider the comments below made by the arts editor of a major West Coast newspaper on what he sees as the consequences of a top-down approach to one's audience. Referencing the academy (e.g., English professors) to signal issues of an approach to books and reading that is disconnected from the needs and interests of the average reader, for him the issue at stake is the perceived relevance of newspaper reviews. He places some of the blame on reviewers:

We share a huge part of the blame for the decline of book criticism because we are a particular kind of people.

We're a lot of English professors, a lot of certainly English majors, a lot of people that really like a certain kind of literary fiction and history, and it wasn't always what most of our readers wanted to read about, and I think we got very school marm-ish about it.

We were too, you know, "Eat your peas," and readers—we're not their teacher. . . .

If we had done a better job of reporting on books and covering books that they were interested in that we would be more vibrant. We would survive.

While this editor was reflecting on the mistakes that book review sections have made and was not contrasting book reviewing with other forms of criticism, it is noteworthy that he associates the gap between readers' needs and the relevance of book sections with the fact that so many reviewers come from a formal academic background with its own assumptions about what constitutes good literature and interesting literary discourse, which may not align with the interests of the average reader.[22]

The importance of code switching when moving between genres of criticism comes through in the way critics describe the imagined audiences of their reviews. For example, one critic who rejects taking a pedantic tone in her reviews imagines the people who read her reviews as people flipping through the review section first thing in the morning: "They're hurtling past. They have to go to work in about 15 minutes. . . . They don't need a lecture." Instead, it was common for critics to draw an equivalence between themselves and their readers in that they are book lovers. Rather than identifying as an expert, another reviewer explained, "I like to think that I speak for the general reader."

Similar to amateur reviewing, then, critics' qualm with academic-style reviewing in journalistic review outlets is that it fails to serve the needs of the average reader. However, the fault lies not in academic critics' literary competency but an approach to the evaluation of books that threatens to cast serious reading as too rarified as to be irrelevant for the average person.

———————

There is a tension in how critics situate themselves in relation to amateurs on the one side, and academic critics on the other. Part of the concern with reader-reviewers was that although they are drawn from the population of general readers, they are not equipped to serve the needs of the average reader. Specifically, reviewers argue for the value of a more specialized group of people with more specialized knowledge and skills to do the job.

At the same time, we saw that in relation to academics, reviewers articulated a different problem: that academic-style reviewing is so specialized as to border on irrelevant. Specifically, we have seen that critics are wary of overly abstract or theoretical emphases in reviews because these can seem too insular and disconnected from the interests of the average readers. In response, reviewers (including those who work as academics) champion applying a more general lens when writing book reviews to better represent the interests of ordinary readers.

How can we understand the coexistence of these seemingly contradictory impulses? To some degree, this is one of the familiar and recognizable internal inconsistencies of boundary-work.[23] An actor characterizes him- or herself in such a way as to highlight how he or she is different from an other, but these qualities change depending on the particular entity from which one is trying to gain distance. For example, scientists may distinguish what they do from religion by claiming an emphasis on *facts* and *empirics*, but when contrasting science from mechanics emphasize its *theoretical bases*.[24] When distancing themselves from reader-reviewers, critics operate as highly specialized connoisseurs. When distinguishing themselves from academic-styled reviews, journalistic critics represent the Everyman.

At the root of these characterizations is the perceived threat that each type of reviewer poses to journalistic critics' preferred vision of how books should be valued in culture today. Novels are not profane commodities. They are works of art and should be treated accordingly. But neither are they so sacred as to be disconnected from the everyday life of readers. It is from this liminal space between the idiosyncrasies of the Amazon reviewers and the esoteric academic that journalistic reviewers operate and situate the value of not only their review but books in general.

A Fine Balance: Between the Market and the Ivory Tower

Critics situate the value of their reviewing in the maintenance of a space for fiction between the ivory tower, which they characterize as disconnected from daily life, and the marketplace, which treats books as commodities no different from shoes and which subjects them to similarly banal criteria of value. I argue the specific content of these characterizations is the result of the dual nature of book reviewing; specifically, book reviewing is simultaneously understood as a form of *art* criticism on the one hand, and cultural *journalism* on the other.[25] In the upcoming section, I outline how the confrontation of these two institutional logics—art criticism and journalism—shape and constrain how critics view the unique place and value of journalistic reviewing.

Book Reviewing as Art Criticism

In its simplest formulation, art criticism is secondary discourse *about art*. But the relationship between art and criticism is more complicated that it appears. As discussed in chapter 1, critics are examples of cultural consecrators.[26] They are actors imbued with the authority to consecrate some art objects as uniquely worthy or special in relation to others. And they do so through their reviews. Stated differently, our ideas of whether something counts as art is often tied to whether influential actors like art critics discusses it *as art*.

For example, Baumann, a sociologist of culture, studied the ascendance of film from mere "entertainment" to "art" in America.[27] He demonstrates that, alongside organizational and technological innovations, it was critics' intellectualizing discourse in their reviews that was crucial to the successful transformation of film into an art form.[28] Similarly, in his study of the Edinburgh Fringe Festival, Shrum shows how the specific language that critics use when writing their reviews plays a key role in distinguishing between highbrow or lowbrow plays.[29] The implication here is that specialized critical discourse is not required of popular culture since the primary evaluative criterion is entertainment. And being subject to criticism is itself constitutive of the status of art. What these studies demonstrate is that it is not simply the content of a book, movie, or play that dictates whether it will be viewed as artistic or popular fare. It is the shared belief among critics and audiences that some types of work require "serious" attention and discourse that distinguishes highbrow from lowbrow cultural work.[30]

Literary reading is unequivocally a highbrow form of cultural engagement. Indeed, books and reading have a unique place in contemporary culture. Cultural commentators have written about the "civilizing thesis," which emphasizes how reading is often treated as an intrinsically good behavior for individuals and society.[31] Furthermore, Griswold's work on the history of readers reveals that literary reading as a form of recreation has always been practiced by a small and elite minority of the population, which she terms the reading class.[32] Given these historical associations, literary reading is viewed as a socially "honorable" activity.

While art criticism can be described as simply discourse about art, it is also *constitutive* of what counts as art. The status of literary reading as a highbrow activity depends in part on reviewers treating novels seriously by way of the appropriate artistic discourses. The importance of this dependency helps contexualize critics' concerns about the lowbrow criteria amateur reviewers are accused of employing in their reviews. Applying appropriate aesthetic standards when reviewing a book seems straightforward enough; however, critics must balance this specialized endeavor with the more quotidian imperatives of journalism.

Book Reviewing as Journalism

According to Gans's journalistic theory of democracy, the role of journalism is to provide relevant and useful information to citizens so that they can better participate in society.[33] And while newspapers may not continue as the organizational base of book reviewing in the future, this historical institutional context means that many reviewers I interviewed use the meanings, the practices, and beliefs of traditional journalism to contextualize the significance of their book reviewing. When viewing book reviewing as a subset of journalism, then, it should serve the same purpose of providing information to the public about what new books are being published and what new ideas are being circulated as part of the cultural conversation in America. A few critics made explicit the connections between the informative imperative and book reviewing. For example, the following critic drew parallels between book reviewing and other form of journalism in terms of the imperative of providing useful information.

> The essential mission of the newspaper is to present information to an audience that's going to be useful, whether it's about a law that's coming or an accident, or weather or something. It's always predicated on this idea of being useful.
>
> And the same thing kind of trickles over into the arts and culture coverage. A lot of the amateur reviewers who are out there and, I think, a lot of the academics forget that as well, which is why their reviews can seem so narrow and kind of contained in a vacuum.

It's no different whether you're covering a city council meeting or you're reviewing a new John Updike novel.

Here, we see the familiar contrast between amateur and academic forms of criticism, with the primary difference concerning the perceived usefulness or relevance each form has for the general reader. The meaning of usefulness conveyed by this reviewer (that is, information about a law, a city council meeting, or the weather) centers on issues that are relevant to the day-to-day lives of average people—information that individuals may not otherwise know about but that is directly applicable to how people go about their days, both at a very practical level—for example, avoiding a street where there's just been an accident—and at a more general level of awareness, such as about local politics.

Another reviewer similarly draws parallels between what he does when reporting on books and the informative aims of political news reporting:

> In the same way that reading a story about a bill in Congress is not really necessarily going to make every person an activist, a particular book review is not going to necessarily make everybody a reader. But [it] is going to hopefully lead to a more informed citizen.

Again, we see that a key ideal in journalism is the assumption that good reporting provides citizens with the information required to make *informed* decisions.[34] Yet, he also draws parallels between the two kinds of reporting to argue for a particular value and vision of what he is trying to accomplish with his book reviews. Just as the success or goals of an article on politics are not measured or determined by whether the journalist induces a particular action in the reader, such as turning the reader into an activist, neither is the success of a cultural reporter gauged by whether readers subsequently go out and buy books or participate in other cultural art forms. The above comments by critics coincide with the discussion in chapter 4 regarding critics' insistence that they do not write reviews for the purpose of selling books despite the fact that book reviews have an evaluative function. Instead, this critic emphasized the shared goal of journalism, which is to inform people about important public matters.

Book reviewing as a form of cultural journalism dovetails with yet other ideals[35,36] of journalistic practice, including: public service (helping readers learn about new books), immediacy (reporting on newly published books); and ethics (customary norms such as civilian versus critical reading practices, as discussed in chapter 3, or the norms against punching down).

However, the overlap between book reviewing and journalism is imperfect. The principle of autonomy—journalists' independence and ability to speak and publish "freely"—is problematized by many reviewers' close ties to the publishing field as we saw in chapters 4 and 5. Again, reviewing is characterized by a switch-role reward structure wherein many reviewers are themselves novelists who temporarily switch into the reviewer role—and back again. The journalistic value of objectivity also does not map neatly onto the work of book reviewers; subjectivity is an intrinsic part of reviewing (see chapter 3).

Additionally, rather than having a commitment to being value-free, reviews are an opportunity to perform and espouse very specific values for many reviewers. One reviewer articulated the specific way that she enacts her beliefs about how reviewers should write about books—by answering two questions for the general reader in every review she writes: "Number one, would I really like to read this book? And number two, should I read this book even if I don't really want to?" The *want* and *should* of reading are clearly separated, and the latter takes priority. The reviewer expanded further on her response:

> There are certain books that are not entertaining, are not a rip roaring page turner but I feel are important for anyone who cares about the culture . . . [about being] an informed and empathetic and sensitive individual. They probably should read it.
>
> And I think too much of today's literary culture has become overwhelmed by people who think—and this is Amazon's fault entirely—"Oh, I only want to read this if it's fun." . . .
>
> Those kinds of values to me are *false values*. (emphasis added)

Reading for "fun" is assumed to be the modus operandi of amateur reviewers, which this critic identifies as a false value. In contrast, she describes the value of reading—including, or perhaps especially, books that you don't want to read—as a tool for cultivating a kind of self: one that is more informed, empathic, and sensitive.

Through their reviews, then, critics are advancing not only an idea about what constitutes good fiction, but also an explicitly normative ideal about the right way to engage with books and the value of reading (hence, a departure from the value-free ideal of journalism).

Here we see a potential tension between the institutional logics of art criticism, on the one hand, and journalism, on the other. Both are integral to journalistic reviewing. The key challenge for critics is how to make the specialized discourse and preoccupations of fiction reviewing "newsworthy," that is, relevant for readers for understanding the world around them. By framing themselves as journalists, critics also reframe readers as citizens, and their reviews as news. And in keeping with book reviewing in the context of the journalistic agenda, an even more important concern among reviewers is to establish books as belonging to the realm of public concern.

How critics resolved the tension between these specialized artistic imperatives and journalistic imperatives varied. It will come as no surprise that among reviewers who identified with their journalistic backgrounds the information-serving imperatives of book reviews were paramount. Reviewers who primarily identified as authors, first and foremost, emphasized the importance of maintaining a particular standard of aesthetic discourse in reviews. However, by bringing these frames together, in whatever configuration of emphases, critics see their work as arguing for the relevance of fiction—as an art form—for understanding everyday life.

Conclusion

Part of the institutional uncertainty faced by reviewers regards questions about the value of professional review(er)s in today's literary landscape. Much of the debate and commentary about the perceived crises in journalism, and in cultural journalism especially, has been limited to the exogenous economic and technological changes resulting from recent digital transformations, which have unsettled previously taken-for-granted assumptions about the value of such work. But such focuses come at the expense of considering the cultural aspects of the crisis construction of these public narratives.[37] In other words, little attention is paid to the *values* encoded in the work of book reviewers above and beyond the specific literary evaluations they proffer. What we see is that the concerns that critics express are not economic or technological but are fundamentally moral concerns about how we appreciate books and the role that reading plays in our daily lives.

Reviewing is not just a statement about the value of a particular title, but a moral statement about how we should appreciate fiction and the deservingness of literature as a central matter of public concern. The blending of art criticism with a journalistic framework employed by book reviewers enables them to distinguish the value of their work from other types of book discourse. The specific contribution is insisting on fiction's relevance, as an art form, for the daily lives of readers—on similar footing as other forms of news. In this way, the reviewers converge with cultural sociologists in the view that individuals can use cultural objects to solve everyday problems.

With this new understanding, we can see how critics' concerns about the folding of book review sections into general "Entertainment" sections, and the retrenchment of book reviews in newspapers more generally, is not solely a concern about the loss of reviewing jobs. Another interpretation, suggested by the above analysis, is that concerns about folding books into entertainment sections may also be driven by a fear may be that books are losing their status as art objects. Additionally, the declining real estate devoted to book reviews in many traditional newspapers suggests that the conception of books as "newsworthy," as in relevant and useful to the lives of citizens for understanding the world around them, is also in decline.[38]

The existential crisis facing book reviewing is often conceptualized as a problem facing reviewers. But, in fact, questions about the ongoing utility and legitimacy of professional reviews have implications for readers as well. Average readers have a vested (if implicit) interest in the health of book reviewing because this critical attention is also a source of the status and honorability that comes from being a reader. To forgo critics' opinions about books is to forgo the status that accompanies fluency with highbrow culture—which is itself indicated by the need for professional criticism. For as long as the fate of reading and reviewing is entangled, then, constant concern with the demise of reviewing can actually be understood as a reaffirmation of the centrality and cultural status of books.[39]

Chapter 8

Conclusion

The book-review sections as a cultural enterprise are, like a pocket of unemployment, in a state of baneful depression.
—HARDWICK[1] IN *HARPER'S MAGAZINE*, 1959

Without books, indeed, without the *news of such books*—without literacy—the good society vanishes and barbarism triumphs.
—WASSERMAN[2] IN *COLUMBIA JOURNALISM REVIEW*, 2007

WHILE PUBLIC PERCEPTION is that book reviewing is currently in crisis, this is actually more of a perennial concern. Consider, for instance, that the opening quotes lamenting the state of book reviewing are fifty years apart. Yet, the specific content of the crisis narrative varies. While some cultural commentators are alarmed by what they perceive to be the declining quality of book reviewing, others question the relevance and economic viability of traditional book reviewing altogether. Such concerns are not entirely new, but they have likely been exacerbated by commercial and technological pressures exemplified by the impetus to digitization.

Challenges to the traditional organizational bases of reviewing have spurred concern about a corresponding cultural crisis. For some, the greatest threat to the current state of reviewing regards the open borders of the profession and the question of *who counts* as a reviewer—and *what counts* as a review. While for others, threats to reading and reviewing, have sparked broader panics about the diminishing role and proper place arts and culture in contemporary society, including fears about an age wherein "barbarism triumphs," to use Wasserman's term.

In the present analysis, we have moved away from a crisis narrative that results from programmatic ideas about what book reviewing should be to a pragmatic focus on the challenges faced by reviewers in the course of doing the actual work of reviewing. Specifically, the approach of the preceding chapters are analytically anchored in the types of uncertainties that critics confront in the course of writing book reviews, how critics respond to these uncertainties, and how this influences what critics do.

We have observed that book reviewing is a highly uncertain endeavor. Moreover, it involves multiple kinds of uncertainty. In response to the *epistemic uncertainty* inherent in evaluating aesthetic quality, editors and reviewers alike rely on personalized qualities to accomplish their evaluative task. Specifically, we found that what qualified critics for the task of reviewing books were perceived personal affinities between the bibliography and biography of the critic and the work under review as a proxy for a "good match" (chapter 2). Additionally, critics exercised a highly reflexive reading strategy when reviewing in efforts to produce a contextualized evaluation of books that was profoundly specific to critics' reading experiences, yet still useful in creating a more generalized evaluation of the book through the *critical consensus* (chapter 3).

In response to a high degree of *social uncertainty* faced by critics in terms of how their audiences would respond to the judgments rendered in their reviews, when confronted with a range of unpleasant consequences for writing a very critical review, many critics expressed a preference to play nice under such circumstances (chapter 4). In contrast, this tendency was reversed when critics confronted a situation wherein the odds of a retribution were decreased, as they were in the case of writing reviews of superstar authors (chapter 5). The switch-role reward structure is central to understanding why critics imagine the range of consequences of their reviews to take the particular form that they do. But it is ultimately how critics draw on their personal experiences as writers (or more importantly, as reviewees), shared stories about other reviewers' experiences, reflections on the status hierarchy in publishing, and the particular publication in which the review will appear that informs their individual calculus about how they handle writing negative reviews.

Finally, as a result of the high degree of *institutional uncertainty* that characterizes reviewing, the lack of clarity and consensus regarding rules and procedures, critics approach reviewing as part of individually defined professional projects (chapter 6). Absent a clear sense of groupness as reviewers, critics draw on other identities and experiences—particularly those germane to their work as writers—to orient their commitments to reviewing. This also informs their individual ways of resolving the tension that arises between the two institutional logics that characterize journalistic criticism: reviewing as a form of journalism, on the one hand, and as a form of art criticism, on the other (chapter 7).

Common to the preceding chapters is the finding that when confronted with different types of uncertainty, reviewers devise "personalized" responses. By personalized I mean that respondents frame their actions as reviewers—an institutional role of cultural intermediaries—as, essentially, personal decisions as individuals. To be clear, while critics experience the dilemmas of reviewing and their responses to these as individuals problem-solving basis,[3] I argue that this personalized experience is itself a product of the larger social organization of reviewing: specifically, the high levels of epistemological, social, and institutional uncertainty faced by reviewers. In the absence of certainty on how to proceed, critics are left to devise personalized solutions to the challenges that arise throughout the reviewing process. This has two important implications.

First, critics feel that they must rely on their own personal experiences, morals, and calculations to determine how to proceed in the face of various practical and ethical dilemmas in reviewing is an anxiety-producing situation. The lack of formal codes of conduct or a sanctioning professional organization means that the weight of decision-making and any resulting consequences is put on the shoulders of critics as individuals. And this can contribute to a sense of insecurity and vulnerability among individual reviewers. The resulting sense of insecurity may help us understand why many critics, then, do not describe feeling empowered while occupying the relatively powerful role of cultural consecrator and why the book reviewer mentioned at the beginning of this book laughed at the idea of being considered a "tastemaker." Instead, the high degree of uncertainty that characterizes reviewing culminates in feelings of vulnerability throughout various points in the review process. There is thus a decoupling of the structural power of the role of the critic, on the one hand, and the phenomenological experience of being a reviewer, on the other, which I argue is symptomatic of the high levels of uncertainty that characterize this work.

A second implication is that critics' emphasis on personalized problem solving translates to a lack of connection with how their individual actions contribute to broader-level realities of reviewing. A sense of detachment from field-level outcomes in reviewing not only undermines the potential for collective efficacy among critics to make changes in the field of reviewing but also obscures how individual responses may be reproducing the status quo.

Consider, for example, in part 2 of the book, wherein we learned of critics' objection to the superstar dynamics of the publishing world, including the perception that brand-name authors received review exposure they did not necessarily deserve. One hypothetical collectively oriented solution would be to have a group of freelance reviewers take it on themselves to impress on the editorial staff at a review section the importance of distributing review coverage more evenly (or perhaps to argue for giving even more attention to new writers or underrepresented authors). However, we saw that critics rely on individual lines of action to address what they see as the unfair review attention lavished on big-name authors: punching up, but never down, which I argued has the potential to actually recreate the very superstar dynamics that reviewers intend to protest against.

Another issue that has gained a lot of collective attention in publishing is the lack of diversity in review pages. Several of my respondents, for example, reflected on the challenges facing women and minorities in the reviewing world (both as reviewers and as reviewees). But once again, just as many reviewers did not see their individual participation in reviewing as connected to this aggregate-level reality.

For some, the issue of diversity was too big an issue and too disconnected from their individual concerns as reviewers to warrant any action. It was a problem for someone else to address. Others observed that women writers face unique barriers compared to their male counterparts, including getting review attention.[4] But rather than pushing for more inclusion through some collective effort, again I find critics expressing personalized strategies to tackle this broader reality. Specifically, given the belief that women writers get fewer opportunities than men and therefore any opportunity carries that much more weight, a few critics indicated that they actively abstain from reviewing first books by women to avoid potentially having to write a less than glowing review of a woman author. Amounting to an identity and status-based form of playing nice, by refusing to review women's work, these critics were never put in the situation where they were might do injury to writers who are already facing additional hurdles by virtue of their gender.

While the underlying intent of these reviewers is perhaps laudable, what it creates is a situation where there are quantitatively fewer reviewers willing to give attention to books by women. Qualitatively, this practice alters the composition of potential reviewers, which is significant given the importance and nuances of making a "good match" (chapter 2) in the pairing of a critic with a book to ensure the fairness of that review. Hence, critics' individual actions to prevent the further disadvantaging of women authors may be creating other barriers.

It is not the point of these examples to suggest that individual reviewers can single-handedly upend the market forces and organizational inertia that drive the current operations of book review sections. Indeed, social movements scholarship can help us understand why there is good reason for the lack of collective action on these collective problems in reviewing. First, as we saw in previous chapters, there is a lack of *groupness* among reviewers. This lack of collective identity prevents collective action.[5,6] Second, even consensus on the disappointing state of reviewing is not enough to spur action: there must be organizational opportunities.[7] And again, many reviewers are writers who feel subject to the power of book-reviewing apparatuses, rather than that they are active agents intrinsic to the process. For these reasons, I submit that the reviewing field will be particularly resistant to change on the part of critics themselves.

The Future of Reviews

One of the limitations of this study is that I restrict my focus to how critics explain and make sense of their own review practices. However, I have not broached several other pressing issues that may be of interest to some readers, including the impact of these practices on reviewing outcomes (that is, resulting positive or negative reviews, or the valuing of fiction), and including the future of reviewing. In the following section, I attend to these topics and offer some predictions based on my study of the field before turning to scholarly implications.

The Persistence of Playing Nice

The majority of reviews on Amazon.com and BN.com are overwhelmingly positive.[8] During my interviews, some critics argued that even in professional practice there's little point in writing negative reviews and telling readers about ten books they should *not* be reading given the scarcity of book reviews. Others argued that if every review were positive then this would potentially dilute the content of reviews. It is precisely this concern that reviews were too positive and uncritical that Elizabeth Hardwick was writing about in the 1959 excerpt quoted at the beginning of this chapter—again demonstrating that such concerns and are not entirely new to the reviewing world though the immediate reviewing environment may appear quite different. I suggest that concerns about reviews being overly "nice" will persist and be amplified by social media platforms and other technologies that facilitate book talk.

We saw in part 2 of the book (chapters 4 and 5) that reviewers' perceptions of how other writers or industry insiders might react to their evaluations affected their sense of fear or freedom to be openly critical. The proliferation of communication technologies such as Twitter provide new platforms for people to draw attention to and comment on reviews—whether for praise or censure. On the one hand, this fact could make it more worthwhile for critics to take the risk of writing attention-getting reviews—for instance a takedown of a famous author. Many reviewers admit, if with some guilt, that they enjoy reading mean reviews or that mean reviews often generate substantial chatter. On the other hand, this additional scrutiny could intensify the pressures critics feel to "play nice" or to "punch up," as the risk of public and professional shaming is also increased through social media.

Yet social media do not change the variables underlying critics' decision making. This is because the new technology has done nothing to dispel the fundamental uncertainties that shape reviewers practices in the first place and that are described in this book. Therefore, I venture that playing nice will continue to permeate book pages.

The Distinguishing Value of Reviews

A central stake identified in debates about the future of reviews concerns how readers are going to learn about new books moving forward. In a zero-sum scenario, only one form of reviewing would survive: either professional or reader reviews would be the chosen source for people wanting to learn about new books. There is some research suggesting a more complementary relationship between the two forms of reviewing. A study in Flanders reports that readers consult *both* professional and reader reviews when seeking information to guide their decisions about which books are worth reading or and which are not.[9]

I suggest that fully comprehending the changing relationship between professional and reader reviewing requires a more nuanced interrogation of what it means for readers to *learn* about books. In the absence of direct data on readers, let us return to the voices of my respondents for some insight on the topic.

In its most utilitarian form, reading book reviews helps readers find titles they would like to read. Yet this is just one of several tools readers have at their disposal. Alternative means for achieving the same end include getting word-of-mouth recommendations from friends, consulting reader reviews, or relying on algorithms that generate book recommendations based on previous online books purchases. One could argue that these are better ways to find a book tailored to one's reading tastes than relying on professional reviews, especially in light of the findings here that that book reviews are not solely assessments of the book under consideration, but also indexes of the professional tensions, anxieties, and aspirations of the individuals who collectively make up the literary field.

Reading reviews can also be understood as a form of reading itself. Recall that many critics, while acknowledging the evaluative function of reviews, balk at the idea that their reviews serve the sole purpose of recommending books. Underlying their unease with the commercial uses of reviews was a view of reviews as formal pieces of writing to be appreciated as such. Readers enjoy reading books, and ostensibly, some also enjoy reading writing *about* books in the form of reviews.

Reviews thus offer multiple forms of value to readers: some readers may consult reviews to learn about books they will enjoy for the express purpose of selecting books to read; others may read reviews simply for the pleasure of edifying themselves about the larger cultural conversation about books. While the former treat reviews as a tool for deciding how to invest their time and dollars, the latter view reading reviews as an immediate investment in one's cultural knowledge. Just as there are different evaluative criteria for appreciating books, then, we can similarly think of different ways of appreciating

reviews. Rather than being in a competitive or even a strictly complementary relationship, professional and reader reviews can thus be
conceptualized as offering readers distinct use values.

At the same time, one cannot dismiss that traditional book review sections have certainly experienced retrenchment. This growing scarcity of professional review attention will continue to stoke
anxieties about the decline of reading culture. However, the relative
scarcity of the traditional book review may not be an indication of
its fading cultural relevance but have the inverse effect of making
book reviews more precious, and in this way enhancing their cultural
importance. With fewer book reviews being issued, to receive a book
review at all is already speaking volumes, thus lending credence to
the idea that the worst review is no review at all.

Can Anyone Be a Critic?

Finally, another way of approaching the question regarding the relationship between professional and reader reviews regards whether
the ranks of professional reviews may open up to reader-reviewers.
One theme that has preoccupied the literature on the digitization
of review practices is its democratizing effects; in particular, how
online spaces wherein people can share their thoughts on books can
potentially bring a wider range of voices to bear on the question of
what is valuable fiction. And there have been a few instances of book
bloggers and other nonprofessional writers effectively crossing over
from writing about books informally on the internet to reviewing for
mainstream media outlets to gain further legitimacy and a broader
platform. Such cases would seem to substantiate claims about the
democratizing potential of digitization as proof that the borders of
reviewing are truly opening.

We should be cautious, however, in interpreting such crossover
cases as evidence of the democratization of the reviewing field. To
illustrate my point, I sketch two trajectories of crossover cases[10] in
which individuals have made the transition from reviewing on personal blogs to being featured in some of the most prominent and
important review media in the Anglophone publishing field—one in
which the blogger used his blogging presence as a platform to cross
over into more mainstream literary activities entirely; and another in
which the blogger maintained a more hybrid practice of writing about
books in both online and traditional mainstream venues.

THE BLOGGER WHO WENT MAINSTREAM

The first case involves a reviewer who was working in a completely unrelated industry for years before starting his blog as a distraction during his divorce. At the height of its success, his blog counted over fifty thousand readers daily; it offered them commentary on news, essays related to literary culture and local literary events, and, of course, posts about books he was reading. This particular critic was cited by several other of my respondents as an example of how the field of reviewing was opening up and changing as a result of the growth of book blogs and amateur participation in reviewing.

He attributes his entry into the world of print reviewing to the review editor of a daily metropolitan newspaper. The editor was having difficulty pairing a book with the right reviewer (the "good match" idea described in chapter 2) around the same time that the blogger had just written about the same book. After reading the blog post, the editor invited the blogger to adapt the online review for print. The blogger's review was well received, and he went on to field invitations to review for a variety of newspapers. Over time, his posts increasingly included links to reviews he had published in venues beyond his personal blog.

In the decade-long run of his blog, the reviewer acquired an MFA in creative writing and published his first book. He recalled "moments of conscious consideration" regarding the future of his blog, thinking, "I can put my energy into being an internet persona and maintaining my internet personality or I can put my energies into being a good novelist." This individual framed his literary ambition ("being a good novelist") as something that was in tension with his efforts to maintain his "internet persona," with respect to the practical considerations of time and energy. He chose to devote his resources to his literary ambition.

In this case, blogging provided a platform that facilitated this person's increased visibility in the reviewing world and accommodated his stepping not only into the world of reviewing, but also into the world of literary activities more generally, including literary production. After this breakthrough, he ceased focusing on the blog and now evinces a professional background similar to the other reviewers I interviewed. At the time of this writing, his last blog post was several years old. He has also published multiple books, teaches creative writing, and is listed as a contributing editor for another mainstream review outlet.

THE HYBRID REVIEWER

A second trajectory was narrated by a reviewer who describes herself as a book critic and blogger. After receiving a master's degree in English literature and doing some teaching as adjunct faculty, she became interested in freelance writing. At one point, she wrote a few book reviews for several alternative papers, and this crystallized her desire to do more similar work. Unlike in the previous example, in this case the reviewer had already done some reviewing for small local papers but was interested in getting more professionally and formally involved in writing book reviews. She achieved this by becoming more engaged in web-based publishing opportunities.

In her case, the reviewer began working in print before transitioning to work online. But she really rose to prominence writing about books in web-based publications. And it was through her online persona and writing that she came to the attention of an editor at a prominent print-based review outlet and started to get assignments in more mainstream publications.

Currently, this reviewer's blog is updated on what she terms a more "sporadic" basis as now she engages in interviews with authors, writes review for traditional news media, and is busy writing her own books. To date, she has published three books. Here is another example of someone who had an interest in writing book reviews who was able to leverage her online presence to amplify her more regional work and gain attention from other reviewing outlets. Her website identifies her as an author and critic. She is known for her book review work but also for work covering more general news items relating to books, for both popular online-only and regular print outlets. Thus, I describe this reviewer as "hybrid" because she operates in both worlds simultaneously.

What do we learn from crossover cases? The above are examples of web-based reviewers or personalities who were able to cross over into reviewing for traditional print media sources—and influential ones at that. On the surface, then, it appears that the internet is providing new ways for other voices to be heard and become integrated into the larger pool of critical voices connected to reviews. Yet, when we consider in more detail the stories and histories of the people who have crossed over, we see that such opportunities are still limited to individuals who fulfill specific criteria.

First, the mechanism by which these crossovers gained entry into print pages was the same as for other reviewers. While personal blogs or new online review outlets create a broader range of opportunities to become known "commodities" to editors rather than, say, meeting an editor at a book industry party, book review editors remain key gatekeepers determining who will be invited to write a review based on the matching process described in chapter 2. So, while there is a bigger pool of talent from which editors, as important gatekeepers, may be able to find potential reviewers, in practice, the constraints by which selection choices are made (such as the imperative of being known) remains the same and practically constrains the actual pool of would-be reviewers to a relatively small group of individuals.

Second, similar to those recruited to review via more traditional pathways (see chapter 2), the people who are asked to review because of their online blogging experiences are not just avid recreational readers: they too had explicit literary or journalistic affiliations expressed through their pursuit of MFAs in writing, through their publications as authors, or through their work as freelance journalists.

These individuals are aspirational cultural producers, not the Joe-at-the-Coffee-Shop reader often conjured by the idea of "reader-reviewers." As a result of these reviewers' literary or journalistic ambitions, even these crossover cases are likely to be influenced by some of the pressures and considerations identified previously in this book, including concerns emanating from the switch-role reward structure of reviewing.

For these reasons, the internet and new online magazines are perhaps better understood as providing new opportunities for would-be reviewers to become known commodities and to come to the awareness of book review editors; however, to suggest that the internet is enabling a new flow of voices—especially in terms of the voices of average readers—is outside the empirical reality described by these crossover cases. Put differently, the critics' circle remains relatively closed.

Yet if digitalization has not resulted in the total democratization of reviewing, then neither has it culminated in the "the good society vanishing." In many ways, new digital technologies have benefited reading culture in North America because they support institutions that enhance the discussion of books and reading, which in turn keep both the discussion of books and the reading of books salient and valued. Specifically, online book clubs, online reviews outlets, book blogs, and other digital venues have provided new spaces in which readers can congregate, engage in book talk, and reaffirm their identity as readers and their love of books.[11] And while alternative forms of entertainment afforded by technology may result in even fewer readers in the future, technology has also helped the relatively small number of people who do read books to locate each other and find new ways of engaging in book-related activity—including *writing reviews or posting commentary about books online*. It appears that creating reader reviews is part of what it means, for many, to be a reader today.

Beyond Books: Uncertainty as a Way Forward for Understanding Evaluation

How unique is critics' sense of vulnerability to the situation of book reviewing? And what broader lessons, if any, can we draw from our deep understanding of this world of evaluators?

Below I consider these questions from two perspectives: first, in a brief examination of how uncertainty and vulnerability manifest in other case studies of evaluation; and second, by reflecting on how the study of uncertainty contributes to a future research agenda for the sociology of evaluation.

The Case of Restaurant Reviewers: Greater Confidence under High Epistemic Uncertainty

Is the sense of professional peril driven by the high level of epistemic uncertainty inherent to evaluating aesthetic experiences? A look at another type of cultural critic suggests otherwise. Take, for example, Grant Blank's study of restaurant reviewers.[12,13] The restaurant reviewers in Blank's study are similar to book reviewers as they offer descriptive and evaluative commentary of an aesthetic experience: specifically, the dining experience at an individual restaurant. One might argue that the epistemic uncertainty experienced by restaurant reviewers is less than that experienced by book reviewers because food can be objectively burnt, and service can be slow or intrusive. However, as Blank notes, diners nonetheless vary in their expectations and preferences around taste and service. For this reason, epistemic uncertainty is still rather high with respect to restaurant reviews.

Yet, restaurant critics do not appear to evince the same sense of disconnection from the broader valuation process that book reviewers describe in terms of the lack of concrete effects of their reviews: on the contrary, restaurant critics believe that the impact of their reviews and what they put in their reviews matter.[14] Consider, for example, the anecdote of one restaurant critic who decided against reviewing a restaurant in an unsafe neighborhood because the critic did not want readers to go there and be robbed.

The robustness of food reviewers can be understood by bringing the other types of uncertainty to bear on these evaluators. Specifically, their confidence could be seen as the result of high epistemic uncertainty being offset by the relatively lower levels of social and institutional uncertainty they confront. First, regarding social uncertainty, restaurant critics are often anonymous. And while reviewers may face backlash from restaurateurs, they do not face the potential of *retributive reviewing* in the same way that book reviewers do. Second, regarding institutional uncertainty, while literary reading is forecast to be on the decline, interest in food culture and criticism is on the rise.[15]

Additionally, unlike book reviews, food reviews do not share the same historical associations with high-status culture; rather, food reviews are more clearly and comfortably aimed toward the institutional role of providing dining (commercial) recommendations. For this reason, food reviewers are unlikely to face the same degree of existential anxiety as book critics even as an increase in amateur, diner-led recommendations compete for attention with professional food reviews in the form of the *Zagat* dining guide and Yelp reviews. While undoubtedly there is consternation about the growth of such amateur reviewing, the point of this example is that epistemic uncertainty by itself is not predictive or determinate of the feeling of vulnerability observed among book reviewers.

*The Case of Scientific Peer Review:
Another Switch-Role Reward Structure*

To what extent is this sense of vulnerability specific to the fact that book reviewers are part of the peculiarities of inhabiting switch-role reward structure? To answer this question, let us consider another set of evaluators who occupy a switch-role reward structure: scientific peer reviewers.[16]

In the case of academic knowledge making, peer review is the "golden standard" for quality control.[17] For example, a sociology professor, as a producer of sociological knowledge and authorized by a PhD and incumbent expert knowledge, will *switch* into the role of evaluator to review an article or book manuscript of another sociologist based on perceived expertise on a topic. And because of overlapping areas of work and expertise, the evaluator will eventually likely also become the reviewee, having his or her work evaluated by another sociologist in the same community of practice in the future. Peer review is essentially another form of the switch-role reward structure since in many academic fields, it is fellow experts (such as fellow historians or scientists) who are able to arbitrate on the quality of a piece of scholarship.

Unlike the book reviewers in my analysis, however, academics evince considerably fewer personalized solutions in the way they go about their evaluative duties. Epistemic uncertainty is also considerably lower as questions about how one *knows* excellence are quite clearly demarcated: authority of evaluation comes from being an expert, and expertise is based on certifiable knowledge evinced through a PhD and a demonstrated research record. Peer reviewers evaluate not as subjective individuals but as experts representing a particular body of concrete knowledge acquired through formal training. In other words, the epistemic uncertainty academic reviewers face is comparatively low.

Additionally, there is more institutional certainty in academic peer review in terms of what procedures are to be followed, which is also tied to epistemic certainty and established norms of scientific knowledge making.[18] Lamont notes that peer review abilities are part and parcel of the self-concepts of scholars as experts.[19] In contrast, critics describe their competencies as writers as something that they *apply* to the separate task of being a reviewer.

One implication of this alternative evaluative scenario, then, is the importance of attending to how one's evaluator role is held concomitantly with the other roles and identities. At the same time, I do not mean to suggest that there is not epistemic insecurity on the part of academic evaluators: status is likely to attenuate how people evaluate one another's knowledge, and Matthew effects have been observed. However, the point here is that the switch-role reward structure does not automatically engender the same sense of vulnerability that has been observed among book reviewers.

Uncertainty across Evaluators:
Enough Uncertainty to Go Around

The survey of different case studies suggests that epistemic, social, and institutional uncertainties can be observed across variety of evaluative situations. In this section, I will expand on the potential and possibilities for this uncertainty framework in the study of valuation more generally.

In the sociology of valuation, there is a proliferation of case studies cataloguing the various contingencies confronted by social actors grappling with radical quality uncertainty. In the sociology of culture, this includes case studies of people engaged in evaluating physical beauty, wine, art prices, theater performances, and more, each detailing how actors respond to circumstances of radical quality uncertainty. While these rich studies point to the different contingencies that shape or constrain evaluative practices, one weakness is that they are largely disconnected from one another.[20]

This book sets out to provide a rich portrait of how book reviewers perceive and perform the work of assessing novels as another case of symbolic goods. However, I develop this case study with an eye toward creating a more general framework for thinking comparatively about how we value goods. In answer to recent calls for more general theorizing about evaluative processes,[21] I argue that understanding the structuring effect of uncertainty and developing a greater theoretical understanding of different *kinds* of uncertainty is the way forward.[22]

But what is the relationship between these different types of uncertainty? The above discussion is suggestive of how analysis of different forms of uncertainty can be useful for a general analysis of evaluation beyond the current case study. I argue that these types of uncertainty elucidate analytically distinct aspects of the evaluative situation that are inherent to understanding the social machinations that produce or undergird these judgments.

To briefly review, *epistemic uncertainty* refers to unpredictability regarding how evaluators come to "know" the quality of an object. When uncertainty is high, as it is with aesthetic objects, quality is difficult to assess in a definitive way. And as we saw in the case of book, the procedures and technologies used to ascertain or assess quality are highly embodied—in part because of the experiential component of reading (and perhaps aesthetic experience in general). What we learned from attending to epistemic uncertainty in this case study is how view subjectivity as wielded as a form of knowledge making, or as a faculty for knowledge making, rather than simply viewing subjectivity as the *absence* of objective means of assessing quality. Evaluation under circumstances of high epistemic uncertainty are not random, even if they appear chaotic, and thereby no less amenable to study than evaluation under circumstances of low epistemic uncertainty, or "objective" forms of evaluation.[23] Attending both to the degree of epistemic uncertainty encountered by evaluators and to the tools used to respond to these degrees of epistemic uncertainty allows us to avoid binaries of objective and subjective evaluation and, instead, productively focus on the parameters of credible judgments or rules for knowledge making.

Social uncertainty refers to unpredictability regarding how relevant others will respond or react to evaluations in the future, which can impact evaluation in the present. In the case of reviewing, we saw how the impact of the switch-role reward structure has implications not only for who reviews but also for how critics craft their reviews with respect to caution and calculating the perceived risks and benefits of their evaluations.

Institutional uncertainty refers to unpredictability about the degree of consensus or contestation concerning the rules that govern behavior, values, and activity; in other words, the meaning and coherence that anchor the evaluative activity. It draws attention to the fact that analysis should be attentive to the *evaluative frames* that people bring to their work. Evaluative frames refer to the "perceived purpose of an evaluation [that] is a priori to the evaluation itself"[23] yet comes to shape evaluative practices. Put differently, how evaluators attribute meaning to the evaluation (in this case, how reviewers attribute meaning to the act of writing reviews) has concrete implications for how evaluations are conducted or executed. While evaluative frames typically relate to how evaluators perceive the intention undergirding their evaluative activities, I extend this concept to consider the range of *meanings* that evaluators bring to the work of evaluation including how the work relates to individuals' identities or related professional projects. This seems especially important to attend to in cases where institutional uncertainty is high and such meanings are not ready-made but it is left to individuals to fill in the gaps or choose from a selection of potential ideas.

I suggest that these types of uncertainty are *irreducible* to one another because they point to distinct analytical parts of an evaluative situation that are inherent to understanding the social machinations that produce or undergird these judgments. However, of course, they are also related and interplay in reality. Throughout the book we have seen how the high degrees of epistemic, social, and institutional uncertainty characterize book reviewing. Specifically, in the case of book reviewing, each type of uncertainty augments the other: the high *epistemic* uncertainty that characterizes reviewing in terms of who is qualified enables the switch-role reward structure that is the organizational basis for high *social* uncertainty because critics, who are plucked from the realm of writers owing to lack of accreditation, are unsure about the far-reaching consequences of their evaluations.

At the same time, the absence of formalized rules to prohibit inappropriate retaliation (high *institutional* uncertainty) is also at play in facilitating high *social* uncertainty. Yet, as we saw in the case of restaurant reviews, different dimensions of uncertainty may also offset or attenuate the impacts of one another. For this reason, how exactly each affects evaluation is likely to depend on the mutual configuration of these different types of uncertainty.

Future work may apply this framework to understanding how these dimensions of uncertainty interplay; and how they are concretely confronted by evaluators can be investigated as a way to develop the comparative evaluative agenda.

———————

We live in a culture of evaluation.[24] Evaluation, in its many forms, has become an ubiquitous part of our everyday lives, and even part of our leisure activities. Yet, the evaluations we produce and consume do not simply reflect and "objective" reality: they active shape and are shaped by and that of key intermediaries, like critics.

Evaluations not only permeate, but also structure our daily lives because they often have distributional consequences, whether in the form of symbolic rewards, what we read, what we buy, or whom we hire. Given their consequential nature, it is therefore important that we understand the different sets of considerations and social machineries that undergird the evaluations that increasingly permeate our everyday lives. How do evaluative decision get made? Who do we trust to make these decisions and why? What are the bases for evaluative decisions? And now, what does the power to evaluate *feel* like and how does this inform the evaluative process?

This book aimed to explore the social processes and practices by which evaluations are produced by focusing on a single set of evaluators: book reviewers. As we learn from this book, the evaluations themselves—such as those inscribed in reviews are only one part of a longer story. To fully understand an evaluation, we also need to understand evaluative practice, which requires attending to evaluators' sense-making of how and why they do what they do. This is not to say that evaluators wield absolute influence, like kings or queens issuing edicts; nor to imply that evaluation is arbitrary. Instead, the portrait of book reviewers that emerges from this study points to how the *fact and feeling of power can be decoupled*, and this is integral to understanding how individuals subsequently wield the power of their positions.

Many questions have been raised about the continued legitimacy of traditional experts and evaluators. In today's culture of evaluation, ambivalent attitudes are encoded in the oft-heard refrain that "Everybody's an expert" or its sister lament "Everyone's a critic." Indeed, this issue of deference—whose opinions and recommendations should be trusted—has been described as "the pressing intellectual problem of [our] age."[25] Yet, this book points to another fundamental issue that has not been adequately addressed. The sense of security among evaluators, not in terms of their status with relevant audiences,[26] but in terms of whether evaluators feel empowered or imperiled by the content, relations with others, and meanings that frame their evaluation work. Such entanglements are crucial for our understanding of how evaluators work, how evaluations get produced, and thus how value gets made.

Acknowledgments

THANK YOU to the people who first saw life and promise in this project: Shyon Baumann, Vanina Leschziner, and Michèle Lamont. Your early and continued support laid the ground for developing the book and my voice as a scholar.

Many people provided useful comments on the various incarnations (as conference proceedings, memos, and stand-alone articles) of what would ultimately form the chapters of this book. I acknowledge the contributions of Stefan Beljean, Clayton Childress, Angèle Christin, Matt Clair, Jeff Denis, Bonnie Erickson, the many members of the ISF Group at Harvard Sociology, Neil McLaughlin, Ben Merrimen, Mark Pachucki, Matt Patterson, Kim Pernell-Gallagher, RFS Seminar Participants at Erasmus School of Media, History, Culture and Communications (Pauwke Berkers, Janna Michaels, Kees Van Rees, Alex van Venrooij, Marc Verboord), the Sandwich Club (Bart Bonikowski, Larissa Buchholz, Maggie Frye, Kimberly Hoang, Ya-Wen Lei), Désirée Waibel, Alex Winter, Queenie Zhu, and two anonymous reviewers. Thanks also to Anita Chong for tolerating my random email, text, and phone consults.

I also am grateful to the editors at Princeton University Press for their confidence in this book project. Meagan Levinson has operated as a North Star on the project, guiding it to maturity amid storms of anxiety and perseverating on my part. My thanks to Samantha Nader for reading so much opaque text and cheerleading me on to eventual cogency. And thanks to Jacqueline Delaney for comments on readability and helping the message of the book land with readers.

My gratitude goes to the people who helped me care for my son (Chongs, Mataks, and Lynches) once he came into the world so that I could continue my writing while also parenting: the two great loves of my life. Grayson, look! Your name is in this book! No, it's not referring to just any Grayson. It's about you: Grayson Ellis Chong-Matak. This must mean you are very, very special.

Thanks to Adam Matak, who knew me capable of this feat before anyone else. Thanks to Agatha and Peter Chong. I hope this book and all the life that led up to this opportunity let you know that your choices and sacrifices to provide your daughters with an education were noticed and honored. Congratulations to eight-year-old me who knew she had a book inside her to share but didn't know about what.

And thank you, finally, to the book reviewers who took the time to share their experiences with me. Each conversation was so intimate and delightful and stays with me to this day. Your stories, candor, and willingness to express vulnerability are truly what made this book possible.

Notes

CHAPTER 1. INTRODUCTION

1. Hirsch, 1972.
2. Ekelund and Borjesson, 2002.
3. Van Rees, 1983.
4. Wendy Werris, "'L.A. Times' Cuts Review Freelancers," *Publishers Weekly*, July 27, 2011. https://www.publishersweekly.com/pw/by-topic/industry-news/promotionalss/article/48139-l-a-times-cuts-review-freelancers.html.
5. Claire Kirch, "Chicago Sun-Times Drops Regular Book Coverage," *Publishers Weekly*, July 1, 2013. https://www.publishersweekly.com/pw/by-topic/industry-news/promotionalss/article/58050-chicago-sun-times-drops-regular-book-coverage.html.
6. John Maher, "Changes in 'New York Times' Books Coverage, Explained," *Publishers Weekly*, March 2, 2017. https://www.publishersweekly.com/pw/by-topic/industry-news/publisher-news/article/72916-changes-in-new-york-times-books-coverage-explained.html.
7. Reader-reviewers write about the widest possible range of books and genres, including those typically excluded from newspaper coverage, including self-published novels, so-called chick lit, and other genres deemed outside the literary mainstream, as well as the range of newly published novels one would find reviewed in journalistic criticism.
8. Verboord, 2011.
9. Bourdieu, 1993.
10. Hellman and Jaakkola, 2012.
11. Bourdieu, 1993; Janssen and Verboord, 2015
12. Bourdieu, 1993.
13. This typology is offered to us in Van Rees, 1983.
14. Berkers, 2009; Van Rees, 1989.
15. Griswold, 1987.
16. Briefly, UK reviewers emphasized a stylistic reading, West Indian reviewers emphasized themes of personal and civic identity, and American reviewers focused on race relations in the books. Griswold (1987) takes this as evidence that the novels (and other cultural objects) do not have a stable set of meanings. Instead, how literary critics interpreted the novels was informed by the broader "social presuppositions" of their national context: for example, America's national preoccupation with race may have influenced American critics' race-relation readings of Lamming's work.
17. Corse and Griffin, 1997.
18. Corse and Westervelt, 2002.
19. Van Rees, 1983.

20. See Berkers et al., (2014) and Verboord (2014) for book examples; and see Kersten and Bielby (2012) and Shmutz and Faupel (2010) for example from studies of film reviewers.
21. See Menger (2014) and Shapin (2012) for exceptions.
22. Cf. Karpik, 2010.
23. Velthuis, 2005.
24. Mears, 2011.
25. Cattani et al., 2014.
26. Antal et al., 2015.
27. Lamont, 2012.
28. Akerlof, 1978.
29. Dequech, 2011.
30. Karpik, 2010.
31. Aspers, 2007.
32. Beckert et al., 2017.
33. Karpik, 2010.
34. Mears, 2011.
35. One of the few other studies that examines the process of critics is Wesley Shrum's (1996) study of the Fringe Festival, which included interviews with critics on site; however, even here, the interview data is used to answer "the question of whether reviewers say what they think" (18) and uses interview data as a proxy for "what they think" and compares it with published reviews and the "expressed opinions of the reviewers themselves." Indeed, this is a tactic used to avoid the issue of asking critics whether "they 'slant' their reviews," which is seen as difficult to address directly. I am asking critics about their process and the different considerations involved in their work. And as the reader will learn, in chapter 6, critics do reveal that they do "slant" their reviews, which points to the fecundity of an interview-based approach to this case study.
36. Karpik, 2010.
37. Dequech (2011) distinguishes between "weak" and "strong" uncertainty in terms of individuals' ability to produce probability of outcomes. The distinction between strong and weak, as I mean it, more closely resembles Dequech's distinction between "ambiguity" and "fundamental uncertainty." It is also related to Knight's (1921) distinction between "risk" (low epistemic uncertainty) and "uncertainty" (high epistemic uncertainty).
38. Karpik, 2010.
39. Lamont, 2012, 211.
40. Blank, 2006.
41. Blank, 2006, 29.
42. Cf. Blank, 2006.
43. Campos-Castillo and Hitlin, 2013, 168.
44. This bears similarities to Beckert's (2013) idea of fictional expectations of how evaluations will bear out consequences in future.
45. This is akin to Knight's (1921) conception of "risk."
46. Crane, 1976.
47. The specific configuration of answers to these questions has been shown to be consequential for the types of innovations that are subsequently produced in an industry, in terms of variety and diversity (Crane, 1976). I explore book reviewing as a reward structure, but rather than focusing on its impact on the types of books that get written or published, I focus on how the social organization of reviewing as a reward structure constrains and enables how book reviewers write their reviews. In other words, I also treat book reviewers as the cultural producers of interest.
48. Friedland and Alford, 1991.

49. Swidler, 1986.
50. One of the challenges I faced was how to construct a sample of such an amorphously defined group when there are no formal criteria or regulations for determining who the members are. I began by generating a list of names of everyone who had published at least one fiction review in one of three major national papers (which I do not identify in order to protect the anonymity of my respondents) that were selected through a combination of criteria including having among the largest circulation numbers; having comparable readership demographics; and having a reputation for arts/culture reviewing. After deleting for multiple entries, this generated a list of over one thousand names of people from which I began random sampling.
51. Although I used only three publications to generate my initial population of reviewers, all my informants have reviewed for multiple publications. Therefore, each critic whose experiences are represented in this study reflects a broad range of editorial input and matching practices, not just the preferences, biases, or idiosyncrasies of a single editorial staff. Additionally, reviewers represent multiple nations in terms of their biographical backgrounds as well as their having experience writing for review outlets in multiple countries, including Canada and the UK, though I am unable to make any cross-national generalizations about reviewing from my data.
52. Pugh, 2013.
53. Rosen, 1981.

CHAPTER 2. HOW REVIEWING WORKS

1. Verboord, 2011.
2. While in the past it was more common for book reviewers to pitch potential review titles themselves to editors or editorial teams, this is less likely to happen today.
3. It is common practice for editors to also write reviews. Some editors write reviews not only for their own pages, but for other review outlets as well. The overlapping of professional roles played by individuals in the world of reviewing is discussed further in later chapters. However, the roles are separate enough that when I interviewed respondents who have worked as editors and reviewers, I asked them to reflect on their experiences as discrete roles when possible.
4. Thompson, 2013.
5. Childress, 2017.
6. Hirsch, 1972.
7. Janssen, 1997.
8. Janssen, 1998.
9. Ridgeway, 2014.
10. Journalistic reviewing outlets typically privilege novels that can be classified as general fiction and occasionally genre fiction such as mystery or science fiction titles.
11. Davis, 1971.
12. Lamont, 2009.
13. DiMaggio, 1982.
14. Chong, 2018.
15. Chong 2013
16. Even though taste is subjective, there are still rules and attempts to work with subjectivity in a rational way. For more on this, see Chong, 2013.
17. Chong, 2013
18. See Lazarsfeld and Merton (1954) and McPherson et al., (2001).
19. Childress and Nault (2019) observe a similar matching logic earlier on in the publishing process as well. Chong, 2013.

20. Rivera, 2016. In some ways, the good match is like the idea of cultural fit discussed in sociology. However there are some important distinctions. Rivera demonstrates how cultural fit, which she describes as perceived similarities based on how one presents oneself, personal histories, and leisure activities, refers to ideas conventionally thought of as cultural capital, and which are held to be important for evaluating job candidates. But such cultural capital, or pursuits and self-presentation, is understood as *distinct* or *separate* from the actual skills and aptitudes needed for the work in question. What we see in this chapter, however, is that in the case of book reviewers, such cultural attitudes or tastes *are* the skill required to do the work. It's about how taste, as an evaluative faculty, is a deeply and intrinsically *incorporated* or embodied type of skill. The openness required to offer a fair evaluation is part of the skill of being a good book reviewer. In this case, the cultural fit *is* the skill, which serves to underscore the connection between personal experiences and the idea of professional qualification. And this is so because the task is understood to be experiential or deeply incorporated. And the tool or instrument reviewers use to evaluate the book is understood as embodied.
21. Shen, 2015.
22. Rivera, 2016.
23. Shen, 2015.
24. The arguments for why this is so are multiple, including the idea of the state authorizing who gets to be called a journalist clashing with the liberal ideologies of the free press (cf. Waisbord 2013; Schudson and Anderson 2009).
25. The idea of closure comes from Weber's discussion in *Economy and Society* (1978) describing how groups draw boundaries between themselves (insiders) and others (outsiders). Applied to the study of work and occupations, closure concerns the ability to define who can legitimately engage in particular work, which is a major stake in any occupational field, as what becomes closed off is a particular market niche or defines the ability to provide a professional service like reviewing (or accounting, or practicing medicine, and so on).
26. Fourcade, 2010, 570.

CHAPTER 3. ACCOUNTING FOR TASTE

1. Shapin, 2012.
2. In *Science in Action*, Latour (1987) follows the production of scientific "facts" (i.e., black-boxing processes). These include trials of strength that test the relation between instruments and the scientists who interpret their data. Scientists are meant to report on whatever facts and data their instruments reveal. But if a critic (or "dissenter") can show that a researcher's interpretation has been distorted by some kind of subjectivity, then the scientist is revealed as a "subjective individual" rather than an "objective representative" of the empirical world (78).
3. Another point of similarity was the concern expressed by many critics about how to accurately and fairly represent a novel. As one critic noted: "You also don't want to put a quotation in that, though it seems to fit your sort of thesis, the quotation isn't representative in a way." Social scientists will recognize the familiar concern with representativeness and not cherry-picking data.
4. These criteria were arrived at inductively and broadly coincide with formal qualities of writing.
5. Abrams, 1993.
6. An author's ability to fulfill genre expectations can sometimes be subsumed under considerations of characterization, plot and structure, and language. However, I

have opted to pull out this dimension from the others because of the unique way that critics cited this feature of the books they reviewed.

7. DiMaggio, 1987, 441.
8. Karpik, 2010.
9. H. Becker, 1982.
10. Hsu, 2006.
11. Statement is informed by interviews with critics and editors.
12. H. Becker, 1982.
13. See also Lamont, 2009, 166.
14. Van Rees, 1987.
15. Goffman, 1956.
16. Turner and Stets, 2005.
17. Baumann, 2007.
18. Thompson (2013) similarly visualizes publishing as a production chain in which each link facilitates the process of getting new books into the hands of the reading public. He notes that the publishing chain is at once a supply chain and a value chain: each subsequent link is supposed to add some value to the final product. The first link in the chain is an author who produces a manuscript. This manuscript may attract the attention of a literary agent (second link) who works with the author to develop the work and sell it to a publishing house (a third link), and so on.

CHAPTER 4. REVIEWING AS RISKY BUSINESS

1. Shrum, 1991.
2. Cf. Chong, 2019.
3. The terminology of switch- and fixed-role markets is given to us by Aspers (2007; 2008), who explains that in fixed-role markets, individuals identify with only one market role, as with fashion designers who are decidedly *producers* of fashion. In a switch-role market, however, individuals switch seamlessly between multiple roles. Another example of a switch-role market is day trading wherein individual traders switch from the role of buyer to seller multiple times over a single day. And Aspers (2008) rightly uses these ideas to sensitize us to the importance of incorporating actors' identities and their phenomenological experience to understand how markets work. However, I use the term "switch-role" to understand how actors' experiences within market structures and their implications for valuation differ in two ways from the above approach. First, Aspers's emphasis on switch-role structures is formally defined in terms of actors who switch roles seamlessly, in part because they do not identify with either side of the market as buyer or seller. In contrast, I use the switch-role idea to draw attention to a case wherein actors absolutely do identify with one role more than another role: in this case the role of cultural producer over that of the reviewer role. Second, I merge these insights with an explicit concern with reward structures (Crane, 1976); and in doing so I illustrate how this switching from one role (cultural producer) to another (evaluator) produces frictions that influence how critics subsequently inhabit and enact their power as cultural consecrators. I refer to this social organization of the literary field as a *switch-role reward structure*. In this reward structure, individuals are invited to switch from their roles as cultural producers to the role of critic (or cultural gatekeeper).
4. Chong, 2015.
5. Shrum, 1996.

6. Using the world of scientific peer review as her case study, Lamont (2009) argues that we need to move beyond considerations of self-interest (i.e., maintaining or improving one's position in the academic field) to examine the neglected aspects of evaluation, including how evaluators understand their role and the emotional consequences of their work. These neglected aspects include the feelings of pleasure and the validation of their self-concepts that emerge from being fair judges and experts whose opinions matter. My interviews suggest that people's core (i.e., nonprofessional) self-concepts as "nice" people also matter.

7. Sgourev and Zuckerman (2011) note that sometimes a sense of loyalty to others can lead people to incorporate other people's interests into their own. The example they use is when academics overcommit their time to teaching duties at the expense of their research activities, although the latter is far more important for their overall career trajectory. But their doing so would cause few people to argue that fulfilling the identity and principle of serving students is ignoble, so that the perceived nobility is enough to entice an academic to perhaps act again in this way—actions that may be seen from the outside and from an instrumental perspective as irrational.

8. Casanova, 2004.

9. The famous story goes that American novelist, journalist, and essayist Norman Mailer either punched or head-butted writer and critic Gore Vidal over a particularly unkind book review.

10. This "classic thing" is an example of what is called sock-puppeting, which, in the case of book reviewing, is when fake identities are used to inflate the numbers of positive or negative reviews of books. In 2004, Amazon.com accidentally listed the identities of many thousands of anonymous posters, and many instances of sock-puppeting were revealed. See Harmon (2004) for details.

11. According to an item reported by the *Guardian* (Flood, 2012), Amazon.com had removed book reviews written by fellow novelists because of suspected "sock-puppeting," which in the case of book reviewing, is when fake identities are used to inflate the number of positive or negative reviews of books.

12. Aspers, 2010.

13. Becker, 1982.

14. Beckert, 2013, 222.

CHAPTER 5. AIM FOR THE STARS: PUNCHING UP, NEVER DOWN

1. Rosen, 1981.

2. A closely related concept is the "winner-takes-all" market, which is a type of reward structure in which the majority of prizes are located at the top and shared by a small group of individuals. However, the mechanisms of the "winner-takes-all" market are different. In this market, small differences in effort and ability are what give rise to the large differences in rewards because of the nature of the jobs that are performed. Put differently, it is the nature of the job that provides some lever by which people can capitalize on small differences in skill. For example, selling shoes versus selling stocks and bonds (cf. Frank and Cook, 1995).

3. Analysis presented here of retail-to-date (RTD) figures of fiction titles released in January 2007 are derived from *Nielsen Bookscan* data.

4. The average number of books published per reviewer at the time of writing was four books (including nonfiction). Of course, the number of books that a person publishes is an imperfect measure or proxy for gauging the fame or status of a writer. One can imagine a situation where authors may publish only one or two books but still be incredibly popular.

5. *New York Times*, http://www.nytimes.com/2009/07/18/books/18martel.html.

6. Some reviewers felt that information about movie deals and the size of an author's advance were too extraneous to take into consideration when writing a review (in particular the reception phase discussed in chapter 3)—yet the status of the authors nonetheless did come into play during this latter portion of the review process described here.

7. Rosen, 1981.

8. Correll et al., 2017, 299.

9. This is also similar to what has been described in science studies as the *Matthew effect*. First proposed by Merton in the sociology of science, the Matthew effect broadly describes the tendency for rewards and resources to flow to parties that already have them. The concept is drawn from the Gospel of Matthew: "For unto every one that hath shall be given, and he shall have abundance: but from him that hath not shall be taken away even that which he hath" (qtd. in Merton, 1968, 53). The Bible verse is Matthew 25:29. In Merton's original usage, this effect has been demonstrated in terms of the disproportionate amount of credit that some scientists receive in part because of their high status. This has also been demonstrated in the evaluation of academic research proposals: academics associated with high-status universities are more likely to be seen favorably, offsetting potential substantive concerns (resulting in a more positive evaluation than might otherwise be given; see also Lamont, 2009, 227, and Hahl and Zuckerman, 2014).

10. The tale "The Emperor's New Clothes" tells the story of a king who parades naked in front of his subjects. Yet, no one in the crowd points out this obvious fact—save for a small boy—for fear of being seen as stupid or incompetent, as all, including the emperor, had been told that only a particular caliber of people would be able to see the clothing.

11. Hahl and Zuckerman, 2014.

12. Rosen, 1981.

13. J. Berger et al., 2010.

14. Note, however, that the general logic this critic outlines—his comfort with being explicitly negative when doing so would not injure the author under review—still broadly fits the trend described in this chapter.

15. Hahl and Zuckerman, 2014, 512.

16. Such an emphasis on competition and re-creating one's social position within the literary field through review is in line with Bourdieusian (1996) expectations.

CHAPTER 6. I AM NOT A CRITIC

1. This was less of an issue for respondents with full-time positions, for review editors, or for people with decades of history writing reviews.

2. Brubaker and Cooper, 2000.

3. Journalism has been described as a particularly "porous" occupation, as Lowrey (2006) notes: "There is no licensure, and though there are schools of journalism, they need not be accredited, it is not required that the occupational group sanction them, and it is common for news organizations to hire individuals without journalism degrees" (256).

4. Lamont et al., 2016.

5. I follow Lamont et al. (2016), in their study of groupness from the perspective of individuals in terms of self-identification and sense of distance or closeness from in- and out-group members.

6. Shrum, 1996.

7. The situation is similar, not only for other arts reporters but for journalists more generally: there is no formal credentialing process for practice. The arguments

for why this is so are multiple, including that the idea of the state authorizing who gets to be called a journalist clashes with the liberal ideologies of the free press (cf. Waisbord, 2013; Schudson and Anderson, 2009). Yet, the boundaries of book reviewing are particularly porous and ill defined even compared with other types of journalism. This is evinced by the steady turnover of people from such a variety of backgrounds who write reviews. In contrast, business, sports, and science reporters, for example, represent a relatively more professionalized and closed-off group of journalists (Marchetti, 2005).

8. Reasons for resistance to accreditation is in part because respondents understand the work of reviewing as an interpretive art, not as a craft, the latter of which is usually associated with rote activities or other similar exercises. Osnowitz (2010) also observes resistance toward accreditation among freelance copywriters and editors for similar reasons. This situation also relates to what we saw in chapter 2, that many of the traits required to be a successful reviewer (and journalist) are noncertifiable.

9. Keen, 2008, 36.

10. Few individuals make a living from being a reviewer; however, most of the people I interviewed were engaged in the literary field in some capacity whether it was as educators or as writers. The concern was that amateur reviews were not vetted or did not confront the same kind of norms and standards that professional reviewers' work did. Although critics may write only five reviews in a given year, the rest of their time is spent in the world of books and ideas. Many reviewers emphasized the difference between themselves as people who "make a career of thinking about [literature]" and amateurs who participate in book culture as a hobbyist and recreationalist. People who emphasized this difference are either novelists, full-time faculty at universities, or journalists, showing that they took very seriously the professional ethics that came along with the duty of reviewing.

11. This critic is referring to the online magazine Salon.com, and one of its cofounders, Laura Miller, who is known for her book criticism both online (i.e., at Salon and in *Slate* magazine) in print (in the *New York Times Book Review* and the *LA Times*).

12. Becker, 1982.

13. Bourdieu, 1993.

14. The idea that it takes ten thousand hours to become an expert was popularized in Malcolm Gladwell's book *Outliers: The Story of Success* (2008).

15. A 2003 report published by the National Arts Journalism Program reveals that articles featuring staff bylines went from 51.6 percent in 1998 to 45.8 percent in 2003, representing almost a 6 percent drop over only a five-year period; and outsourcing arts coverage to newswire services and syndicators or freelancers is also on the rise. So the world of books is not being singled out for extinction. However, the dwindling fate of many stand-alone book review sections makes clear a pattern of retrenchment.

16. Christin, 2014.

17. Caves, 2000.

18. Menger, 2014.

19. Menger, 1999.

20. Menger, 2014, 124.

21. Leah Price (2007) has noted that narratives concerning the "crisis" and declining state of reading in America typically make fine distinctions about types of reading. Furthermore, the National Endowment for the Arts 2004 report "Reading at Risk: A Survey of Literary Reading in America" reveals that literary reading is at risk in America.

22. Baumann, 2007.

23. H. Becker, 1978.
24. Bourdieu, 1984.
25. Griswold, 2008.
26. Bourdieu, 1986.
27. G. Becker, 1994.
28. Swartz, 1997, 2.
29. Bourdieu, 1986.
30. Frenette, 2013.

CHAPTER 7. DO WE NEED BOOK REVIEWS?

1. Jaakkola, 2015, 538.
2. M. Berger and Beder, 1998.
3. Elkins and Engelke, 2003.
4. Rubenstein, 2006.
5. McDonald, 2007.
6. Pool, 2007.
7. Elkins and Newman, 2008.
8. Connelly, 2007.
9. Wasserman, 2007.
10. Wilby, 2008.
11. Cf. Hardwick, 1959.
12. Breese, 2016.
13. Jackaway, 1995.
14. Davies, 2006.
15. Gans, 1974.
16. The distinction between entertainment and aesthetic value also echoes Bourdieu's (1984) characterization of popular and aesthetic dispositions. Though Bourdieu was focused on the homology between class-based ways of appreciating highbrow and lowbrow cultural goods, here we are not making claims about class. Again, people who read the types of books that are reviewed in mainstream outlets (i.e., literary fiction) are very likely to be of high socioeconomic backgrounds (Griswold et al., 2005).
17. Baumann, 2007.
18. H. Becker, 2007.
19. Baumann, 2007.
20. Verboord, 2014.
21. Chong (2019) documents how professional reviewers alter their reviewing practices when moving between traditional review outlets and less formally organized blogs or web publications. She argues the difference is one of epistemic styles rather than competency.
22. This editor's comments coincide with what Jaakkola (2015) identifies as the "elitization" crisis frame, which views an ivory-tower ethos as harming cultural journalism.
23. This emphasis on *selected* characteristics draws attention to the fact that boundary-work involves making distinctions between "us" and "them"; and actors may choose to present themselves, their work, or their group in ways that best align with their own interests (Gieryn, 1983, 782; see also Lamont and Molnár, 2002.
24. Gieryn, 1983, 786.
25. Hellman and Jaakkola (2012) note the tension between what they call the aesthetic and the journalistic paradigms within cultural journalism more generally as

expressed by arts reviewers and reporters, respectively. What the present analysis reveals is that these paradigmatic tensions can be observed within the *reviewer* role alone.

26. Bourdieu, 1996.
27. Baumann, 2007.
28. Specifically, Baumann (2007) found that around the 1960s, film critics began integrating the specialized vocabulary typical of literary reviews, whose "status as an art form has long been established" (156–57) when writing about films. The persuasiveness of this argument is made all the more compelling by the fact that the shift in how critics wrote about films was *not* caused by qualities of the films themselves.
29. Shrum, 1996.
30. Shrum explains, "This difference in mediative capacity is in large part what we *mean* by high-status art forms. 'Serious' works are those works about which critical talk is relevant" (1996, 9; italics in original).
31. Griswold et al., 2005.
32. Griswold, 2008.
33. Gans, 1974.
34. Jacobs and Townsley, 2011.
35. Deuze, 2005.
36. Hellman and Jaakola, 2012.
37. Alexander et al., 2016.
38. Schudson and Anderson, 2009.
39. Breese (2016) makes a similar argument about the perennial concern regarding news journalism.

CHAPTER 8. CONCLUSION

1. Hardwick, 1959.
2. Wasserman, 2007 (emphasis added).
3. On *individualized* solutions, cf. Beck, 1992; Giddens, 1991.
4. Verboord, 2011.
5. Taylor and Whittier, 1992.
6. Polletta and Jasper, 2001.
7. Raeburn, 2004.
8. Chevalier and Mayzlin, 2006.
9. Verboord, 2011.
10. These case studies are drawn from Chong, 2018.
11. Long, 2003.
12. Blank, 2006.
13. Data is drawn from Grant Blank's (2006) study of restaurant reviewers. The restaurant critics studied by Blank are cultural journalists or critics who were writing for newspapers. In this way, they bear similarities to the book reviewers in this study as they are writing for general consumers of generalist publications; they review fine dining (not everything gets reviewed, such as chain restaurants, similar to how books in certain popular genres tend not to get reviewed); and they are serving a general audience. These food critics are also embedded in the editorial structure of a newspaper.
14. Popular essays are concerned with things like fraud and the overwhelming impact of services such as Yelp, but not with the "death" of food criticism in the same way that people write about book reviews.
15. Johnston and Baumann, 2014.

16. Lamont, 2009.
17. Lamont, 2009.
18. Cf. Merton, [1942] 1973.
19. Lamont, 2009.
20. Lamont, 2012.
21. Lamont, 2012.
22. Pierre Michel Menger (2014) has written about the fruitfulness of using uncertainty to study artistic production; the difference here is that I define uncertainty in more detail, and I restrict it to what is derived from the experiences of actors themselves. Additionally, I am both expanding and contracting the generalizability of the framework. First, I am limiting its utility to evaluation (its own form of cultural production). Second, I suggest that we can expand this framework to evaluation contexts outside of the realm of cultural production where epistemic uncertainty is high.
23. See also Shapin (2012) and Menger (2014) for more on this point.
24. Additionally, Espeland et al. deploy the term "evaluation culture" to describe our society as one that is "obsessed with ratings, indicators, and performance measures of all sorts" (2016, 172). This trend has been noted by cultural anthropologists and economic sociologists, who have coined such concepts as "audit culture" (Strathern, 2003) to describe how the logic of auditing—a practice of monitoring and measuring performance taken from the world of finance—has come to be applied to other social arenas in the name of improving accountability and transparency.
25. Collins and Evans, 2002, 237.
26. Bourdieu, 1993.

Bibliography

Abrams, M. H. (1993). *A Glossary of Literary Terms*. Fort Worth, TX: Harcourt Brace College Publisher.

Ahrens, Frank. (2009). "The Accelerating Decline of Newspapers." *Washington Post*, October 27. http://www.washingtonpost.com/wp-dyn/content/article/2009/10/26/AR2009102603272.html.

Akerlof, G. A. (1970). "The Market for 'Lemons': Quality Uncertainty and the Market Mechanism." *Quarterly Journal of Economics* 4 (3): 488–500.

Alexander, J. C., Breese, E. B., and Luengo, M. (Eds.). (2016). *The Crisis of Journalism Reconsidered*. New York: Cambridge University Press.

Antal, A. B., Hutter, M., and Stark, D. (2015). Moments of Valuation. *Exploring Sites of Dissonance*. Oxford: Oxford University Press.

Asad, A. L., and Bell, M. C. (2014). "Winning to Learn, Learning to Win: Evaluative Frames and Practices in Urban Debate." *Qualitative Sociology* 37 (1): 1–26.

Aspers, P. (2007). "Theory, Reality, and Performativity in Markets." *American Journal of Economics and Sociology* 66 (2): 379–98.

———. (2008). "Analyzing Order: Social Structure and Value in the Economic Sphere." *International Review of Sociology* 18 (2): 301–16.

———. (2010). *Orderly Fashion: A Sociology of Markets*. Princeton, NJ: Princeton University Press.

Baumann, S. (2007). "A General Theory of Artistic Legitimation: How Art Worlds Are Like Social Movements." *Poetics* 35 (1): 147–65.

Beck, U. (1992). *Risk Society: Towards a New Modernity*. Vol. 17. Thousand Oaks, CA: Sage.

Becker, G. S. (1994). "Human Capital Revisited." In *Human Capital: A Theoretical and Empirical Analysis with Special Reference to Education*, 15–28. 3rd ed. Chicago: University of Chicago Press.

Becker, H. S. (1978). "Arts and Crafts." *American Journal of Sociology* 83 (4): 862–89.

———. (1982). *Art Worlds*. Berkeley: University of California Press.

Beckert, J. (2013). "Imagined Futures: Fictional Expectations in the Economy." *Theory and Society* 42 (3): 219–40.

———. (2016). *Imagined Futures*. Cambridge, MA: Harvard University Press.

Beckert, J., and Musselin, C. (Eds.). (2013). *Constructing Quality: The Classification of Goods in Markets*. Oxford: Oxford University Press.

Beckert, J., Rössel, J., and Schenk, P. (2017). "Wine as a Cultural Product: Symbolic Capital and Price Formation in the Wine Field." *Sociological Perspectives* 60 (1): 206–22.

Berger, J., Sorensen, A. T., and Rasmussen, S. J. (2010). "Positive Effects of Negative Publicity: When Negative Reviews Increase Sales." *Marketing Science* 29 (5): 815–27.

Berger, M., and Beder, S. (Eds.). (1998). *The Crisis of Criticism*. New York: New Press.

Berkers, P. (2009). "Ethnic Boundaries In National Literary Histories: Classification Of Ethnic Minority Fiction Authors In American, Dutch And German Anthologies And Literary History Books, 1978–2006". *Poetics 37* (5–6):419–438.

Berkers, P., Janssen, S., and Verboord, M. (2014). Assimilation into the literary mainstream? The classification of ethnic minority authors in newspaper reviews in the United States, the Netherlands and Germany. *Cultural Sociology* 8(1), 25–44.

Blank, G. (2006). *Critics, Ratings, and Society: The Sociology of Reviews.* Lanham, MD: Rowman and Littlefield.

Bourdieu, P. (1984). *Distinction: A Social Critique of the Judgement of Taste.* Cambridge, MA: Harvard University Press.

———. (1986). "The Forms of Capital." In *Cultural Theory: An Anthology*, Szeman, I., and Kaposy, T. (eds.). Malden, MA: Wiley Blackwell, 81–93.

———. (1993). *The Field of Cultural Production: Essays on Art and Literature.* New York: Columbia University Press.

———. (1996). *The Rules of Art: Genesis and Structure of the Literary Field.* Stanford, CA: Stanford University Press.

Breese, E. B. (2016). "The Perpetual Crisis of Journalism: Cable and Digital Revolution." *Fudan Journal of the Humanities and Social Sciences.* 8(1): 49–59.

Brubaker, R., and Cooper, F. (2000). "Beyond 'Identity.'{~?~ thinspace}" *Theory and Society* 29 (1): 1–47.

Campos-Castillo, C., and Hitlin, S. (2013). "Copresence: Revisiting a Building Block for Social Interaction Theories." *Sociological Theory* 31 (2): 168–92.

Casanova, P. (2004). *The World Republic of Letters.* Cambridge, MA: Harvard University Press.

Cattani, G., Ferriani, S., and Allison, P. D. (2014). "Insiders, Outsiders, and the Struggle for Consecration in Cultural Fields: A Core-Periphery Perspective." *American Sociological Review* 79 (2): 258–81.

Caves, R. E. (2000). *Creative Industries: Contracts between Art and Commerce.* Cambridge, MA: Harvard University Press.

Chevalier, J. A., and Mayzlin, D. (2006). "The Effect of Word of Mouth on Sales: Online Book Reviews." *Journal of Marketing Research* 43 (3): 345–54.

Childress, C. (2017). *Under The Cover: The Creation, Production, And Reception Of A Novel.* Princeton, NJ: Princeton University Press.

Childress, C., & Nault, J. F. (2019). "Encultured Biases: The Role of Products in Pathways to Inequality". *American Sociological Review*, 84(1): 115–141.

Chong, P. (2011). "Reading Difference: How Race and Ethnicity Function as Tools for Critical Appraisal." *Poetics: Journal of Empirical Research on Culture, the Media and the Arts* 39 (1): 68–84.

———. (2013). "Legitimate Judgment in Art, the Scientific World Reversed? Maintaining Critical Distance in Evaluation." *Social Studies of Science* 43 (2): 265–81.

———. (2015). "Playing Nice, Being Mean, and the Space in Between: Book Critics and the Difficulties of Writing Bad Reviews." In *Moments of Valuation: Exploring Sites of Dissonance*, Antal, A. B., Hutter, M., and Stark, D. (eds.). Oxford: Oxford University Press.

———. (2019). "Valuing Subjectivity in Journalism: Bias, Emotions, and Self-Interest as Tools in Arts Reporting." *Journalism* 20 (3) 427–33.

———. (2018). "Openness as a Means to Closure." In "The M in CITAMS@30." Spec. issue, *Studies in Media and Communications* 18:99–119.

Christin, A. (2014). "Clicks or Pulitzers? Web Journalists and Their Work in the United States and France." PhD diss., Princeton University.

Collins, H. M., and Evans, R. (2002). "The Third Wave of Science Studies: Studies of Expertise and Experience." *Social Studies of Science* 32 (2): 235–96.

Connelly, M. (2007). "The Folly of Downsizing Book Reviews." *Los Angeles Times*, April 29. http://www.latimes.com/la-op-connelly29apr29-story.html.

Correll, S. J., Ridgeway, C. L., Zuckerman, E. W., Jank, S., Jordan-Bloch, S., and Nakagawa, S. (2017). "It's the Conventional Thought That Counts: How Third-Order Inference Produces Status Advantage." *American Sociological Review* 82 (2): 297–327.

Corse, S. M., and Griffin, M. D. (1997). "Cultural Valorization and African American Literary History: Reconstructing the Canon." *Sociological Forum* 12 (2): 173–203.

Corse, S. M., and Westervelt, S. D. (2002). "Gender and Literary Valorization: The Awakening of a Canonical Novel." *Sociological Perspectives* 45 (2): 139–61.

Crane, D. (1976). "Reward Systems in Art, Science, and Religion." *American Behavioral Scientist* 19 (6): 719–34.

Davies, D. R. (2006). *The Postwar Decline of American Newspapers, 1945–1965*. Westport, CT: Praeger Publishers.

Davis, M. S. (1971). "That's Interesting! Towards a Phenomenology of Sociology and a Sociology of Phenomenology." *Philosophy of the Social Sciences* 1 (2): 309–44.

Dequech, D. (2011). "Uncertainty: A Typology and Refinements of Existing Concepts." *Journal of Economic Issues* 45 (3): 621–40.

Deuze, M. (2005). "What Is Journalism? Professional Identity and Ideology of Journalists Reconsidered." *Journalism* 6 (4): 442–64.

DiMaggio, P. (1982). "Cultural Entrepreneurship in Nineteenth-Century Boston: The Creation of an Organizational Base for High Culture in America." *Media, Culture and Society* 4 (1): 33–50.

———. (1987). "Classification in Art." *American Sociological Review* 52 (4): 440–55.

Drewry, J. E. (1966). *Writing Book Reviews*. Boston: The Writer.

Ekelund, B. G., and Borjesson, M. (2002). "The Shape of the Literary Career: An Analysis of Publishing Trajectories." *Poetics* 30:341–64.

Elkins, J., and Engelke, M. (2003). *What Happened to Art Criticism?* Chicago: Prickly Paradigm.

Elkins, J., and Newman, M. (2008). *The State of Art Criticism*. New York: Routledge.

Espeland, W. N., Sauder, M., and Espeland, W. (2016). *Engines of Anxiety: Academic Rankings, Reputation, and Accountability*. New York: Russell Sage Foundation.

Flood, A. (2012). "Amazon Removes Book Reviews by Fellow Authors." *Guardian*, December 12. https://www.theguardian.com/books/2012/nov/05/amazon-removes-book-reviews.

Fourcade, M. (2010). "The Problem of Embodiment in the Sociology of Knowledge: Afterword to the Special Issue on Knowledge in Practice." *Qualitative Sociology* 33 (4): 569–74.

Frank, R. H., and Cook, P. J. (1995). *The Winner-Takes-All Society*. New York: Penguin.

Frenette, A. (2013). Making the Intern Economy: Role and Career Challenges of the Music Industry Intern. *Work and Occupations* 40 (4): 364–97.

Friedland, R., and Alford, R. R. 1991. "Bringing Society Back In: Symbols, Practices and Institutional Contradictions." In *The New Institutionalism in Organizational Analysis*, Powell, W. W., and Dimaggio, P. J. (eds.), 232–67. Chicago: University of Chicago Press.

Gans, H. (1974). *High Culture and Popular Culture: An Analysis and Evaluation of Taste*. New York: Basic Books.

Garfinkel, H. (1967). *Studies in Ethnomethodology*. Cambridge, UK: Prentice-Hall.

Giddens, A. (1991). *Modernity and Self-Identity: Self and Society in the Late Modern Age*. Stanford, CA: Stanford University Press.

Gieryn, T. F. (1983). "Boundary-Work and the Demarcation of Science from Nonscience: Strains and Interests in Professional Ideologies of Scientists." *American Sociological Review* 48 (6): 781–95.

Gladwell, M. (2008). *Outliers: The Story of Success.* New York: Little, Brown.

Goffman, E. (1956). "Embarrassment and Social Organization." *American Journal of Sociology* 62 (3): 264–71.

Gorman, E. H., and Sandefur, R. L. (2011). "'Golden Age,' Quiescence, and Revival: How the Sociology of Professions Became the Study of Knowledge-Based Work." *Work and Occupations* 38 (3): 275–302.

Griswold, W. (1987). "The Fabrication of Meaning: Literary Interpretation in the United States, Great Britain, and the West Indies." *American Journal of Sociology* 92 (5): 1077–117.

———. (2008). *Regionalism and the Reading Class.* Chicago: University of Chicago Press.

Griswold, W., McDonnell, T., and Wright, N. (2005). "Reading and the Reading Class in the Twenty-First Century." *Annual Review of Sociology* 31:127–41.

Guetzkow, J., Lamont, M., and Mallard, G. (2004). "What Is Originality in the Humanities and the Social Sciences?" *American Sociological Review* 69 (2): 190–212.

Habermas, J. (1991). *The Structural Transformation of the Public Sphere.* Cambridge, MA: MIT Press.

Hahl, O., and Zuckerman, E. W. (2014). "The Denigration of Heroes? How the Status Attainment Process Shapes Attributions of Considerateness and Authenticity." *American Journal of Sociology* 120 (2): 504–54.

Hardwick, E. (1959). "The Decline of Book Reviewing." *Harper's Magazine*, October. https://harpers.org/archive/1959/10/the-decline-of-book-reviewing/.

Harmon, A. (2004). "Amazon Glitch Unmasks War of Reviewers." *New York Times*, February 14. https://www.nytimes.com/2004/02/14/us/amazon-glitch-unmasks-war -of-reviewers.html.

Hellman, H., and Jaakkola, M. (2012). "From Aesthetes to Reporters: The Paradigm Shift in Arts Journalism in Finland." *Journalism* 13 (6): 783–801.

Hirsch, P. M. (1972). "Processing Fads and Fashions: An Organizational-Set Analysis of Culture Industry Systems." *American Journal of Sociology* 77:639–59.

Hsu, G. (2006). "Jacks of All Trades and Masters of None: Audiences' Reactions to Spanning Genres in Feature Film Production." *Administrative Science Quarterly* 51 (3): 420–50.

Jaakkola, M. (2015). "Witnesses of a Cultural Crisis: Representations of Media-Related Metaprocesses as Professional Metacriticism of Arts and Cultural Journalism." *International Journal of Cultural Studies* 18 (5): 537–54.

Jackaway, G. L. (1995). *Media at War: Radio's Challenge to the Newspapers, 1924–1939.* Westport, CT: Praeger.

Jacobs, R. N., and Townsley, E. (2011). *The Space of Opinion: Media Intellectuals and the Public Sphere.* Oxford: Oxford University Press.

Janssen, M.S.S.E, & Verboord, M.N.M. (2015). Cultural Mediators and Gatekeepers. In *International Encyclopedia of the Social Sciences and Behavioral Sciences. Second Edition* (pp. 440–446).

Janssen, S. (1997). "Reviewing as Social Practice: Institutional Constraints on Critics' Attention for Contemporary Fiction." *Poetics* 24 (5): 275–97.

———. (1998). "Side Roads to Success: The Effect of Sideline Activities on the Status of Writers. *Poetics* 25:265–80.

Johnston, J., and Baumann, S. (2007). "Democracy versus Distinction: A Study of Omnivorousness in Gourmet Food Writing." *American Journal of Sociology* 113 (1): 165–204.

———. (2014). *Foodies: Democracy and Distinction in the Gourmet Foodscape.* Princeton, NJ: Princeton University Press.

Karpik, L. (2010). *Valuing the Unique: The Economics of Singularities.* Princeton, NJ: Princeton University Press.

Keen, A. (2007). *The Cult of the Amateur: How Today's Internet Is Killing Our Culture.* New York: Doubleday, 2007.

Kersten, A., and Bielby, D. (2012). "Film Discourse On The Praised And Acclaimed: Reviewing Criteria In The United States And United Kingdom". *Popular Communication* 10 (3): 183–200.

Knight, F. H. (1921). *Risk, Uncertainty and Profit.* New York: Hart, Schaffner, and Marx.

Lamont, M. (2009). *How Professors Think.* Cambridge, MA: Harvard University Press.

———. (2012). "Toward a Comparative Sociology of Valuation and Evaluation." *Annual Review of Sociology* 38 (1): 201–21.

Lamont, M., and Molnár, V. (2002). "The Study of Boundaries in the Social Sciences." *Annual Review of Sociology* 28 (1): 167–95.

Lamont, M., Silva, G. M., Welburn, J., Guetzkow, J., Mizrachi, N., Herzog, H., and Reis, E. (2016). *Getting Respect: Responding to Stigma and Discrimination in the United States, Brazil, and Israel.* Princeton, NJ: Princeton University Press.

Latour, B. (1987). *Science in Action: How to Follow Scientists and Engineers through Society.* Cambridge, MA: Harvard University Press.

Lazarsfeld, P. F., and Merton, R. K. (1954). "Friendship as a Social Process: A Substantive and Methodological Analysis." *Freedom and Control in Modern Society* 18 (1): 18–66.

Lena, J. C., and Peterson, R. A. (2008). "Classification as Culture: Types and Trajectories of Music Genres." *American Sociological Review* 73 (5): 697–718.

Leschziner, V. (2015). *At the Chef's Table: Culinary Creativity in Elite Restaurants.* Stanford, CA: Stanford University Press.

Leidner, R. (2016). Work Identity without Steady Work: Lessons from Stage Actors. In *Research in the Sociology of Work*, 3–35. Wagon Lane, Bingley: Emerald.

Long, E. (2003). *Book Clubs: Women and the Uses of Reading in Everyday Life.* Chicago: University of Chicago Press.

Lowrey, W. (2006). Mapping the Journalism-Blogging Relationship. *Journalism* 7 (4): 256.

Marchetti, D. (2005). "Subfields of Specialized Journalism." In *Bourdieu and the Journalistic Field*, Benson, R., and Neveu, E. (eds.), 64–82. Malden, MA. Polity.

McCormick, L. (2015). *Performing Civility: International Competitions in Classical Music.* Cambridge: Cambridge University Press.

McDonald, R. (2007). *The Death of the Critic.* Ann Arbor: University of Michigan Press/Bloomsbury Academic.

McPherson, M., Smith-Lovin, L., and Cook, J. M. (2001). "Birds of a Feather: Homophily in Social Networks." *Annual Review of Sociology* 27 (1): 415–44.

Mears, A. (2011). *Pricing Beauty: The Making of a Fashion Model.* Berkeley: University of California Press.

Menger, P. M. (1999). "Artistic Labor Markets and Careers." *Annual Review of Sociology* 25 (1): 541–74.

———. (2014). *The Economics of Creativity.* Cambridge, MA: Harvard University Press.

Merton, Robert K. (1968). "The Matthew Effect in Science." *Science* 159: 53–63.

———. ([1942] 1973). "The Normative Structure of Science." In *Sociology of Science: Theoretical and Empirical Investigations*, 273 Chicago: University of Chicago Press.

Nell, V. (1988). *Lost in a Book: The Psychology of Reading for Pleasure.* New Haven, CT: Yale University Press.

Osnowitz, D. (2010). *Freelancing Expertise: Contract Professionals in the New Economy.* Ithaca, NY: Cornell University Press.

Phillips, D. J., and Zuckerman, E. W. (2001). "Middle-Status Conformity: Theoretical Restatement and Empirical Demonstration in Two Markets." *American Journal of Sociology* 107 (2): 379–429.

Polletta, F., and Jasper, J. (2001). "Collective Identity and Social Movements." *Annual Review of Sociology* 27:283–305.

Pool, G. (2007). *Faint Praise: The Plight of Book Reviewing in America.* Columbia: University of Missouri Press.

Price, L. (2007). "You Are What You Read." *New York Times,* December 23. https://www.nytimes.com/2007/12/23/books/review/Price-t.html.

Pugh, A. (2013). "What Good Are Interviews for Thinking about Culture? Demystifying Interpretive Analysis." *American Journal of Cultural Sociology* 1 (1): 42–68.

Raeburn, N. C. (2004). *Changing Corporate America from Inside Out: Lesbian and Gay Workplace Rights.* Minneapolis: University of Minnesota Press.

Ridgeway, C. L. (2014). "Why Status Matters for Inequality." *American Sociological Review* 79 (1): 1–16.

Rivera, L. A. (2012). "Hiring as Cultural Matching: The Case of Elite Professional Service Firms." *American Sociological Review* 77 (6): 999–1022.

———. (2016). *Pedigree: How Elite Students Get Elite Jobs.* Princeton, NJ: Princeton University Press.

Rosen, S. (1981). "The Economics of Superstars." *American Economic Review* 71 (5): 845–58.

Rubenstein, R. (2006). *Critical Mess: Art Critics on the State of Their Practice.* Lennox, MA: Hard Press Editions

Satzewich, V. (2015). *Points of Entry: How Canada's Immigration Officers Decide Who Gets In.* Vancouver: University of British Columbia Press.

Schmutz, V., and Faupel, A. (2010). "Gender And Cultural Consecration In Popular Music". *Social Forces* 89(2): 685–707.

Schudson, M., and Anderson, C. (2009). "Objectivity, Professionalism, and Truth Seeking in Journalism." In *The Handbook of Journalism Studies,* Wahl-Jorgensen, K., and Hanitzsch, T. (eds.), 88–101. New York: Routledge

Sgourev, S. V., and Zuckerman, E. W. (2011). "Breaking Up Is Hard to Do: Irrational Inconsistency in Commitment to an Industry Peer Network." *Rationality and Society* 23 (1): 3–34.

Shapin, S. (2012). "The Sciences of Subjectivity." *Social Studies of Science* 42 (2): 170–84.

Shen, J. (2015). "A Third Type of Job Search Behavior: The Use of the Formal-Informal Joint Channel in Matching Individual Qualifications with Hiring Requirements in Urban China." *Journal of Chinese Sociology* 2 (1): 3.

Shrum, W. (1991). "Critics and Publics: Cultural Mediation in Highbrow and Popular Performing Arts." *American Journal of Sociology* 97 (2): 347–75.

———. (1996) *Fringe and Fortune.* Princeton, NJ: Princeton University Press.

Strathern, M. (2003). "Introduction. New Accountabilities: Anthropological Studies in Audit, Ethics and the Academy. In *Audit Cultures,* 13–30. New York: Routledge.

Swartz, D. (1997). *Culture and Power: The Sociology of Pierre Bourdieu.* Chicago: University of Chicago Press.

Swidler, A. (1986). "Culture in Action: Symbols and Strategies." *American Sociological Review* 51 (2): 273–86.

Taylor, V., and Whittier, N. (1992). "Collective Identity in Social Movement Communities: Lesbian Feminist Mobilization." In *Frontiers in Social Movement Theory,* edited by A. D. Morris and C. M. Mueller, 104–29. New Haven, CT: Yale University Press.

Thompson, J. B. (2011). *Merchants of Culture: The Publishing Business in the Twenty-First Century.* Cambridge, UK. Polity.

Turner, J. H., and Stets, J. E. (2005). *The Sociology of Emotions.* Cambridge: Cambridge University Press.

Van Rees, C. J. (1983). "How a Literacy Work Becomes a Masterpiece: On the Threefold Selection Practised by Literary Criticism." *Poetics* 12 (4–5): 397–417.

———. (1987). "How Reviewers Reach Consensus on the Value of Literary Works." *Poetics* 16:275–94.

———. (1989). "The Institutional Foundation Of A Critic's Connoisseurship." *Poetics* 18:179–198.

Velthuis, O. (2005) *Talking Prices: Symbolic Meanings of Prices on the Market for Contemporary Art*. Princeton, NJ: Princeton University Press.

Verboord, M. (2009). "The Legitimacy of Book Critics in the Age of the Internet and Omnivorousness: Expert Critics, Internet Critics and Peer Critics in Flanders and the Netherlands." *European Sociological Review* 26 (6): 623–37.

———. (2011). "Cultural Products Go Online: Comparing the Internet and Print Media on Distributions of Gender, Genre and Commercial Success." *Communications* 36 (4): 441–62.

———. (2014). "The Impact of Peer-Produced Criticism on Cultural Evaluation: A Multi-level Analysis of Discourse Employment in Online and Offline Film Reviews." *New Media and Society* 16 (6): 921–40.

Waisbord, S. (2013). *Reinventing Professionalism: News and Journalism in Global Perspective*. Cambridge, UK: Polity.

Wasserman, S. (2007). "Goodbye to All That." *Columbia Journalism Review* 46 (3): 43.

Weber, M. (1978). *Economy and Society: An Outline of Interpretive Sociology*. Vol. 1. Berkeley: University of California Press.

Wilby, Peter. (2008). "Final Chapter for Book Reviews?" *Guardian*, December 15. https://www.theguardian.com/media/2008/dec/15/telegraph-newspapers-literary-editors.

Wohl, H. (2015). "Community Sense: The Cohesive Power of Aesthetic Judgment." *Sociological Theory* 33 (4): 299–326.

Index

academic reviews and critics, 5, 102, 103, 123–27, 130
aesthetic goods, 8
aesthetic valuation, 6, 7
Amazon.com, 2, 3, 121, 122, 127, 139, 160n10, 160n11
analysis in reviews, 61–63
art criticism: book reviewing as, 128–29; and journalistic reviewing, 132
Aspers, P., 159n3
assymetric information, 7
authors. *See also* writers: superstars, 137
The Awakening God (Chopin), 5

Baumann, S., 128, 164n28
Beckert, J., 81, 156n44
"big books," 20–22, 24, 91
Blank, Grant, 9, 145–46, 164n13
bloggers, 104, 120, 141–45, 163n21
BN.com, 139
book reviewers. *See* reviewers
book reviewing. *See* reviewing
book reviews. *See* reviews
books: "big," 20–22, 24; criteria for review selection, 20–24; as entertainment, 121–22, 133; "interesting," 22–24; sales and reviews, 3–4, 84, 118
Bourdieu, Pierre, 4, 6, 115, 163n16
Breese, E.B., 164n39

capital, 115–16
characters: in fiction, 42–43
Chicago Sun-Times, 2
Chicago Tribune, 73
Childress, C., 157n19
Chong, Phillipa, 163n21
Chopin, Kate, 5
civilian mode of reading, 38–40
closure, 33, 158n25

code language, 69
code switching, 124, 126
connoisseurship, 9–10
Corse, S.M., 5
Crane, D., 156n47
critical consensus, 51–55, 135
critic mode of reading, 40–42
critics. *See* book reviewers
cultural capital, 116, 158n20
cultural consecrators, 4, 128, 136

Davis, M.S., 23
Dequech, D., 156n37
description in reviews, 61

Edinburgh Fringe Festival, 128, 156n35
editor (of book section): as book reviewer, 110, 157n3; choosing books to review, 91–92; choosing reviewers, 32–33, 34, 59, 68, 78; intervention by, 66, 67; as review audience, 60; role of, 63, 66
epistemological uncertainty. *See* uncertainty
essayistic reviews, 4–5, 103–4
evaluation, 150–51; culture of, 165n24; function of reviews, 64–67; literary, 4, 17, 51; and uncertainty, 7–9
evaluative criteria, 42–50

fiction: characters in, 42–43; evaluation criteria for, 42–50; genres, 47–49; literary, 23–24, 48, 163n16; plot and structure in, 43–44; relative and absolute yardsticks, 49, 50; themes in, 46–47
fixed-role markets, 159n3
Fourcade, M., 34–35

Galbraith, Robert, 93
Gans, H., 129